T0328665

Cambridge Elements

Elements in Environmental Humanities
edited by
Louise Westling
University of Oregon
Serenella Iovino
University of North Carolina at Chapel Hill
Timo Maran
University of Tartu

DEEP HISTORY, CLIMATE CHANGE, AND THE EVOLUTION OF HUMAN CULTURE

Louise Westling
University of Oregon

CAMBRIDGE
UNIVERSITY PRESS

Shaftesbury Road, Cambridge CB2 8EA, United Kingdom

One Liberty Plaza, 20th Floor, New York, NY 10006, USA

477 Williamstown Road, Port Melbourne, VIC 3207, Australia

314–321, 3rd Floor, Plot 3, Splendor Forum, Jasola District Centre, New Delhi – 110025, India

103 Penang Road, #05–06/07, Visioncrest Commercial, Singapore 238467

Cambridge University Press is part of Cambridge University Press & Assessment, a department of the University of Cambridge.

We share the University's mission to contribute to society through the pursuit of education, learning and research at the highest international levels of excellence.

www.cambridge.org
Information on this title: www.cambridge.org/9781009257336

DOI: 10.1017/9781009257343

First published 2022

A catalogue record for this publication is available from the British Library.

ISBN 978-1-009-25733-6 Paperback
ISSN 2632-3125 (online)
ISSN 2632-3117 (print)

Deep History, Climate Change, and the Evolution of Human Culture

Elements in Environmental Humanities

DOI: 10.1017/9781009257343
First published online: August 2022

Louise Westling
University of Oregon

Author for correspondence: Louise Westling, lhwest@uoregon.edu

Abstract: This Element follows the development of humans in constantly changing climates and environments from *Homo erectus* 1.9 million years ago, to fully modern humans who moved out of Africa to Europe and Asia 70,000 years ago. Biosemiotics reveals meaningful communication among coevolving members of the intricately connected life-forms on this dynamic planet. Within this web, hominins developed culture from bipedalism and meat-eating to the use of fire, stone tools, and clothing, allowing wide migrations and adaptations. Archaeology and ancient DNA analysis show how fully modern humans overlapped with Neanderthals and Denisovans before emerging as the sole survivors of the genus *Homo* 35,000 years ago. Their visions of the world appear in magnificent cave paintings and bone sculptures of animals, and more recently in written narratives like the Gilgamesh epic and Euripides' *Bacchae* whose images still haunt us with anxieties about human efforts to control the natural world.

Keywords: climate change, migrations, cultural development, cave painting, animal haunting

ISBNs: 9781009257336 (PB), 9781009257343 (OC)
ISSNs: 2632-3125 (online), 2632-3117 (print)

Contents

Introduction: Who Are We?

Our species arrived quite recently on the geological scene. Life on Earth is thought to have begun around 3.5 billion years ago, our hominin ancestors in Africa only appearing around 4 million years ago, and our kind of humans coming out of Africa only 70,000 to 50,000 years ago (Leakey 2020: 80, 138, 270–271, 306–332; Reich 2018: 6; Dennell 2009: 13–34; Smail 2008: 9).[1] *Homo sapiens* coevolved with every life-form now on Earth, and many others now extinct. We are literally made of the same elements, sharing genes with plants as well as bacteria, viruses, and all other living creatures. In fact, our bodies are colonies of symbiotic cells and viruses, each body a collective in dynamic cooperation (Yong 2016; Margulis 1998). We are not "strange strangers" as Timothy Morton (2010: 50) would have us believe (see also Clark 2013). We are biological kindred, with the same organs as other mammals. As Darwin (1981) pointed out more than 150 years ago, human fetuses begin looking very much like those of dogs, then develop gradually as they mimic evolutionary change from fish-like creatures with gills and tails to the distinct form of primates and finally human infants (10–17). Understanding this reality must be the central starting point for understanding our place in the living community. In order to think seriously about who we are, and what our future might be as the climate begins a drastic transformation, we need to go back much farther than the few hundred years, or perhaps the few thousand years, commonly reckoned to be our historical heritage, as Daniel Lord Smail (2008: 6–11) urges.

Perhaps, as Dipesh Chakrabarty (2009) asserts, recent climate change has collapsed the Humanist presumption that our species history is distinct from natural history; indeed, he seems to accept the Anthropocene concept that we have become actual shapers of the planet's geology. But the Humanist view is relatively recent, as is the realization of the environmental crisis we have wrought. The notion of the Anthropocene may itself be an expression of human exceptionalism, when a much broader and deeper look at the Earth's history reveals how late and minimal our impacts have been compared to the enormous dynamism of planetary life. Peter Ward and Joe Kirschvink (2015) claim that vast geological changes and planetary catastrophes have driven ecological/environmental change and shaped our relatively short experience as a species. And, indeed, the evolution of ecosystems has been more important

---

[1] The earliest known specimen of *Homo sapiens*, found at Kibish, Ethiopia, is dated at 195,000 years ago (Leakey 2020: 168–169). But see also Ann Gibbons (2017) and Ewen Calloway (2017), who describe very archaic specimens from Morocco, recently dated at 315,000 years old. This latter example is not accepted by some experts as *Homo sapiens* because of its primitive, elongated skull.

than species in arriving at the forms of life we see at present. Most of Earth's past has been violently different from the relatively calm period of present life-forms. "The present is not a key to most of the past," Ward and Kirschvink (2015: 5) write, "Making it so has limited us in our vision and understanding." Others, such as Barry Cunliffe, Robin Dennell, David Quammen, David Reich, Maeve Leakey, and Jeremy de Silva, also consider increasing evidence from paleobiology, archaeology, ancient genome studies, and paleogeography in offering ways to freshly evaluate our experience and cultures.

The following narrative will show how archaic hominins developed before emerging as human-like types that migrated out of Africa, adapting to changing climates and landscapes. We will see how *Homo sapiens* moved into Europe and Asia 70,000 years ago, encountering and interbreeding with other forms of early humans such as Neanderthals and Denisovans. Following this long process will reveal the ways our ancestors created tools and cultural forms that led to our present situation. The final sections of the story will examine the remarkable appearance of sophisticated Paleolithic cave art in western Eurasia, the strange art of Neolithic Anatolian temples and towns, and two examples of archaic literary works that depict the tragic consequences of human efforts to control wild creatures and landscapes.

Premises

To begin exploring this wide sweep of history as the context for our own emergence and flourishing, two main premises should be acknowledged. *First*, this is a story of the development of living forms and their remarkable changes and adaptations to violent environmental events such as volcanic eruptions, earthquakes, atmospheric changes – such as the Great Oxygenation Event of 2.1 billion years ago that poisoned most anaerobic organisms and thus created an atmosphere for oxygen-breathing creatures – and other radical changes in climate. These include two or three periods of Snowball Earth events during which the entire globe was frozen. One lasted from 2.35–2.22 billion years ago, and a succession of others occurred from 717–635 million years ago, imposing severe environmental filters on the evolution of life. No large land animals existed until after these vast changes, which were followed by meteor strikes that wiped out most creatures during the Cretaceous and Permian periods (Ward and Kirschvink 2015: 68–113, 212–224). No mammals resembling humans appeared until 1.9 million years ago with the emergence of *Homo erectus* or *ergaster* (Leakey 2020: 270; Sykes 2020: 36; Dennell 2009: 26–34). We have therefore not been a factor in most of the history of planetary life; the Anthropocene could be seen as an unfortunate blip. As Lynn Margulis

(1998) wrote, "Humans are not even central to life. We are a recent, rapidly growing part of an enormous ancient whole" (120).[2]

Second, my approach will place major emphasis on the active semiosis (or meaningful communication) and sedimentation of information in the Earth and in all living forms. This understanding comes from the interdisciplinary movement of *biosemiotics* that recognizes sign processes as fundamental to life.[3] Biochemist Jesper Hoffmeyer (2008) explained that "the biosemiotics idea implies that life on Earth manifests itself in a global and evolutionary *semiosphere*,[4] a sphere of sign processes and elements of meaning that constitute a frame of understanding within which biology must work" (5). It includes communication in the form of sound, scent, movement, colors, forms, electrical fields, chemical signals, touch, and more. And the continual stream of these sign processes "that regulate and coordinate the behavior of living systems, depends upon the special receptivity that evolutionary systems over time have developed towards selected features of their environment" (Hoffmeyer 2008: 62). Biosemiotics thus assumes that meaningful communication has been part of all life as it has developed over millions of years, dynamically operating in bodies from cells and organs to organisms and communities of organisms such as forests and coral reefs, and that animal communication and specifically human language and culture are extensions of that semiosis. In other words, biosemiotics is central to the history of life.

---

[2] Marco Armiero's (2021) *Wasteocene* Element in this series perhaps offers a better name for our effect on the ecosystem and geology.

[3] Developed independently in Estonia in the late 1970s–1980s (the Tartu–Moscow School) and in Denmark in the late 1980s (the Copenhagen School), this movement has involved biologists, chemists, and linguists who realized that information, and indeed active meaningful communication, lie at the base of living systems, including human culture. In Tartu, cultural linguist Juri Lotman led a group of Estonian and Russian linguists in developing a theoretical approach to cultural semiotics, which became connected with the ecological studies of Kalevi Kull and his collaboration with Hungarian-American linguist Thomas Sebeok in the 1980s. In Copenhagen, biochemist Jesper Hoffmeyer, with a formative interest in ecological history, worked with Claus Emmeche in informational biology to develop a parallel semiotics of nature influenced by the semiotic theory of American philosopher Charles Sanders Peirce (Hoffmeyer 2008: 364–368). By the 1990s, these two loosely related groups began cooperative meetings and projects, including Thomas Sebeok and his studies of nonhuman communication. Hoffmeyer (2008) credits Sebeok with "the broadminded intellect and indefatigable energy to assemble all the threads that would serve as the foundation for the modern biosemiotics project, both intellectually and socially" (364). Younger scholars such as Timo Maran at Tartu (author of the Element on *Ecosemiotics* in this series) and Søren Brier at Copenhagen have become important contributors to the movement, along with Terrence Deacon at University of California–Berkeley. Almo Farina's Element on *Semiotic Landscapes* in this series also reflects his wide-ranging work in the biosemiotics movement. See the special Biosemiotics and Culture issue of *Green Letters: Studies in Ecocriticism* 19 (November 2015) for a collection of presentations by key biosemioticians at a May 2013 conference at the University of Oregon.

[4] Cultural linguist Juri Lotman invented the term and concept of *semiosphere* (Lotman and Clark 2005); the original paper, in Russian, was published in 1984. See also Hoffmeyer (2008: 366).

1 Life Emerges

The earliest forms of life (archaea – ancient cells) were formed by an enclosing lipid membrane which distinguished and protected them from their surroundings while simultaneously remaining in communication with the exterior and controlling most of what happened within the cell. Taking in nourishment and expelling waste, the membrane (cell wall) was originally, and remains, a semipermeable barrier (Noble 2017: 39–51; Hoffmeyer 2008: 25–38; Margulis 1998: 81) that is always responding to and interacting with its environment, clearly in a kind of communication. In effect, "the surface membrane of a unicellular organism is therefore its nervous system" (Noble 2017: 59; see also Margulis 1998: 82–85). Hoffmeyer (2008) explains that "the biological orchestration of an organism is created by a well-tuned symphony of biosemiotic relationships across the membranes which in each instant of an organism's life controls and coordinates the biochemical, physiological, and even cognitive processes that together constitute life" (31). As organisms evolved and proliferated, they profoundly changed the environment (Noble 2017: 49; Lewontin 2000: 53–55, 125–126; Margulis 1998: 107–111). Life is always changing the Earth, as it did so dramatically in the Great Oxygenation Event.

This is the kind of dynamic *Chiasm* or intertwining that French philosopher Maurice Merleau-Ponty (1973) described as the central ontological fact (133–143; see also 114–115). It includes cosmic and geophysical forces, weathers, fluid systems, physical and chemical relationships as well as the interactions of living beings that evolved within those forces on the Earth and are made of the same elements. What distinguishes "life" from "nonlife" is the "aboutness" of living things, their dynamic orientation toward or away from, openness or rejection of, substances and situations and beings according to their own needs. This continuous activity requires agency combined with the interpretation of stimuli from outside the cell or organism. And it implies some kind of intersubjectivity from its beginnings (Hoffmeyer 1996: vii–viii; Wheeler 2016: 158–159). Gradually the necessary communication between inside and outside the first single-celled living things (prokaryotes, without nuclei) began to involve closer relationships, and alliances eventually produced complex cells and new creatures (eukaryotes, cells with nuclei, such as those found in plants, fungi, and animals).

Intersubjectivity must underlie this process, for it involves a profoundly intimate intercorporeality dynamically unfolding between two or more organisms that requires purposiveness, some kind of intentionality, no matter how primitive (Hoffmeyer 2008: 57, 94, 311). Edmund Husserl understood this when he defined various forms of empathy (*Einfühlung* – feeling with another) as the only mode through which animals can have sense. "This subjective element also guides everything in the world that we call organic life" (Husserl 2013: 6). This is not primarily a self-conscious process or one activated by "mind" as we understand it in ourselves or in complex animals like birds or octopuses, whales or primates. Rather, it results from differential energy flows, tendencies toward equilibrium, self-catalyzing and self-organizing properties of chemical systems, attractions to food, or movements away from danger. In larger organisms it develops from experimental play of various kinds and the ways organs evolved to interact and bodily parts to emerge and coordinate as a whole. Hoffmeyer (2008) predicts that biologists and biosemioticians are only at the beginning of discoveries that will reveal "a nearly inexhaustible stock of *intelligent* semiotic interaction patterns taking place at all levels of complexity from cells and tissues inside the bodies up to the scale of ecosystems" (50–51). He thinks that the evolution of species is likely to be dependent on whole systems of semiotic relations within the environment in which organisms are nested. This requires the consideration of a new integrative level between the species and the ecosystem – "i.e., the level of the *ecosemiotic interaction structure*" Hoffmeyer (2008: 195–196). Such research is already well under-way, as Timo Maran (2020) explains so cogently in his Element in this series: *Ecosemiotics: The Study of Signs in Changing Ecologies*. He and his colleague Kalevi Kull have defined ecosemiotics as "a branch of semiotics that studies sign processes as responsible for ecological phenomena" (Maran and Kull 2014: 41).

Symbiosis

Lynn Margulis was the first to introduce the concept of symbiosis as the key evolutionary force for increasingly complex life-forms. Unsatisfied with the rigid neo-Darwinist claims that natural selection and random mutation are the only drivers of organic change, she explored mid-nineteenth-century ideas about the role of symbiosis in the work of such scientists as Konstatin Meresczhkowski, Boris Kozo-Polyansky, and Ivan Wallin, and then discovered the genetic basis for supporting them. "A major theme of the microbial drama," Margulis (1998) wrote, "is the emergence of individuality from the community interactions of once-independent actors. . . . The tendency of 'independent' life is to bind together and reemerge in a new wholeness at a higher, larger level of organization" (11). Such processes result in *symbiogenesis*, "the emergence of new living forms, bodies, organs, and species" (25–26, 33). At first derided and dismissed by mainstream biologists, she persevered and continued publishing more and more studies that began to gain acceptance. Her work has now become the dominant view – she is "the mother of symbiogenesis in evolution," acknowledges Oxford biologist Denis Noble (2017):

> We don't know how rapidly the symbiogenetic events leading to eukaryotes may have happened. A simple stage of ingestion of a bacterium by a prokaryotic cell would have been virtually instantaneous of course: just gobble the goody! But there must have been many other stages. Instead of being eaten up for fuel, the ingested bacterium would have needed to survive inside and prove beneficial to its host, while the host would have needed to be beneficial to the bacterium. We know also that much of the DNA of bacterial origin subsequently moved to the nuclear genome. . . . Only a small amount of DNA now remains in mitochondria and chloroplasts. That would have involved many steps of natural [internal] genetic engineering (204–205).

So it seems that the working inner parts of eukaryotic cells such as organelles, mitochondria, ribosomes, chloroplasts, perhaps even the nucleus, were once free-floating individual creatures. And part of these processes was reorganization of genomes that occurred naturally within organisms as they evolved. Thus, contrary to earlier reductionist emphasis on competition, many leading biologists now see internal agency and cooperation as also being central features of complex dynamics; such a view is obviously congruent with biosemiotics.[5]

All complex organisms contain such networks. Lynn Margulis's (1998) claim that "each one of us is a massive colony of microorganisms" (65) is now well-accepted, with Ed Yong's (2016) book, *I Contain Multitudes: The Microbes within Us and a Grander View of Life* providing a lively description of the present understanding of our situation as well as for many different animal bodies. He explains that most microbes (viruses, bacteria, phages, yeasts, fungi) in our bodies are not pathogens but instead behave like a hidden organ. Human cells have between 20,000 and 25,000 genes, but our symbiotic microbes have around 500 times more. Their genetic richness and adaptability respond to the challenges both outside and within us, helping to digest food, produce vitamins and minerals, neutralize toxins, and attack more dangerous microbes that could cause disease. We now know that they guide in the construction of our organs and educate our immune system, even affecting the development of the nervous system and eventually shaping moods and mental states in some cases. This is true not just for humans but for all animals. Many of those close to us such as mice have similar cooperative arrangements that can be experimentally studied in ways not easily managed for humans. In animals, from elephants to protozoa, microbes help maintain a steady internal environment in multiple

---

[5] But David Quammen (2018) reports that recent work in horizontal gene transfer reveals a number of unwelcome fusions of new genetic material caused by disease or other kinds of invasive conjunctions (336–342). See also Cédric Feschotte (2008).

ways. In mammals, they clean vascular systems, help replenish the linings of gut and skin, affect the storage of fat, and even influence the continual remodeling of skeletal systems. And their presence in our immune systems is a profound and complex communicative network that shapes the system early in life and then works to react to threats by attacking some of them but also calming the body's responses to others (Yong 2016: 11–12, 63–64, 70–71; see also Quammen 2018 336–342).

How did this happen? It would be impossible to recover the exact details of the evolutionary dance of symbiogenesis over more than three billion years, but some possible developments have been hypothesized. Margulis (1998) describes the proposal of "fungal fusion" by two Canadian botanists, K. A. Pirozynski and D. W. Mallock, to help explain the evolution of plants 450 million years ago. They suggested that fungi and algae coevolved in a symbiogenesis that combined them in a mutually beneficial partnership: "Ultimately plants then provided sap for internalized fungi whose mycelial threads developed tough branching and roots" (107–108). This idea was extended by Peter Astatt of the University of California to suggest that by long association, plants adopted and retained fungal genes in their root tissue. It is now well established that mycorrhizae extend in huge networks from the roots of plants, supplying the plants with minerals such as phosphorus and nitrogen (Margulis 1998: 107–108).

More recently, forestry scientist Suzanne Simard (2021) has established how these plant networks communicate in intricate ways, sharing nutrients among various plants "in a web of interdependence, linked by a system of underground channels, where they perceive and connect and relate with an ancient intricacy and wisdom that can no longer be denied. . . . The evidence was at first highly controversial, but the science is now known to be rigorous, peer-reviewed, and widely published" (4–5). Simard has revealed this vast network of fungal life in more than twenty years of experimental work in American and British Columbian forests as well as in laboratories, beginning with her PhD dissertation research in the 1990s and now documented in many scientific publications. These demonstrate how seedling plantations are nurtured by fungal networks made up of varied species that trade sugars and proteins, protect against infections, provide shade to each other, and together create healthy symbiotic ecosystems of insects, bacteria, and other organisms (Simard et al. 2015; Simard et al. 2013; Simard 2012). They define ways in which trees communicate, learn from each other, and pass on information from the past (Simard 2018). Her most recent book makes an analogy between animal neural networks and the movement of chemical information among plants.

Molecules move not just through the cross walls of adjacent plant cells and the end pores of back-to-back fungal cells, but also across synapses at the apices of different plant roots, or different mycorrhizas. Chemicals are released into these synapses, and the information must then be transported along an electrochemical source-sink gradient from fungal-root tip to fungal-root tip, similar to the workings of a nervous system. (Simard 2021: 230).

Jakob von Uexküll (1934)[6] had used the forest as an example of multiple interlocking life-forms and the varied perspectives and activities of its creatures in his *Stroll through the Worlds of Animals and Men*. In *Ecosemiotics: The Study of Signs in Changing Ecologies* in this Elements series, Timo Maran (2020) also uses the forest as a model for the semiotic relations between ecosystems and human culture that parallels Simard's description of the web of life in British Columbian forests. Maran (2020) emphasizes the interconnected structural layers and distributed communication codes involved in ecological meanings that create the rich ecological relationships in the forest (53–58). This astonishingly complex ecosystem could only have coevolved among billions of organisms in mutual responses to each other and their changing environments since life began. This vast mutualism continues to evolve and change in the present. As Merleau-Ponty (1973) asks in *The Visible and the Invisible* concerning our own bodies in relation to the wider living world, "why would this generality, which constitutes the unity of my body, not open it to other bodies? ... Why would not the synergy exist among different organisms if it is possible within each? Their landscapes interweave, their actions and their passions fit together exactly" (142).

An example of mutualism still underway is the bladderwort described by Hoffmeyer, a carnivorous plant commonly found in freshwater lakes. This plant feeds on zooplankton that in turn graze upon the *periphyton*, a film of bacteria, diatoms, and blue-green algae that covers the leaves of the plant and attract bacteria like the zooplankton. In this indirect mutualism all the involved species benefit from the arrangement. Even as the bladderwort nourishes itself by eating the zooplankton, the zooplankton at the same time gain great benefit from the opportunity to graze upon the phytoplankton layer. For its part, the phytoplankton layer profits by broadening its living space when the bladderwort's surface area increases. Thus, by ensuring the bladderwort's growth, the periphyton increases its own biomass, even through the process in which it is itself eaten (Hoffmeyer 2008: 47–48). Moreover, the situation is even more complex, because larger creatures such as ducks, muskrats, and turtles eat bladderworts

---

[6] This translation is used instead of the more recent one because it retains the crucial use of the word *Umwelt* in the particular way Uexküll intended, whereas it is omitted in the later version.

and, at the same time, when the plant flowers it emits a sweet nectar that draws insect pollinators.

All this symbiotic reality has developed over billions of years with what can only have been complex intersubjective processes increasingly discovered by biological research in recent years, as we have seen. In *The Symbiotic Habit*, Angela E. Douglas (2010) shows that symbiosis is everywhere around us in coevolutionary biological alliances that include whole ecosystems that are both antagonistic and cooperative, "with the increasing evidence that the reciprocal interactions in many associations are not played out in highly specific relationships between two partners but are diffuse, involving groups of similar species with similar benefits" (162–163).

Examples of plant–animal coevolution at a more visible scale are the myriad relationships between flowering plants and insect pollinators. Darwin guessed at the symbiotic bond between the Madagascar orchid *Angraecum sesquipedale* and its pollinator when a friend sent him an example of the orchid in 1862. This blossom has a nectary a foot long, and Darwin predicted that large moths must exist in its environment with a proboscis capable of extending to a length of between ten and eleven inches (25.4–27.9 cm) (Darwin 1862: 197–203). When this prediction was published, the idea was ridiculed. However, in 1907 such a Madagascar moth was discovered. Yet, not until 1992 was the evidence for such a partnership observed (Ardetti et al. 2012). First recorded with an infrared camera at night in the jungle of Madagascar, it is now viewable on YouTube ("Darwin's comet orchid" 2008).

This example of a pollinator coevolving in collaborative development to accord with the material/formal needs of a plant is unusually dramatic, but all around us are myriads of insects, birds, and mammals whose intimate associations with plants have evolved to provide benefits for both participants. Obviously, both reproductive and nutritive connections are involved in these relationships, because the plants are sedentary and need to be fertilized or have pollen or seeds dispersed beyond their limited areas, whereas the pollinators are mobile and thus must be attracted to the plants and choose which ones offer appropriate nourishment. The honeybee gathers nectar from flowers and also collects pollen from the stamen (male reproductive part) which she then takes to other flowers where some of it rubs off on the pistil (female part) and thus fertilizes the plant, but all in the bee's purposive collecting of food for the hive. In many cases, ants disperse seeds, but inadequate research has been focused on this mutualism to date. Indeed, Judith L. Bronstein, Ruben Alarcón, and Monica Geber (2006) explain in an extensive summary study that plant–insect mutualism "was not a prominent concept in ecology or evolutionary biology through most of the 20th century" (5). Natural history studies of such phenomena were common from the mid-nineteenth century, however, with a particular focus on important agricultural mutualisms such as bee pollination of food crops.

At the present relatively early stage of research into the evolution of a wider range of pollination mutualisms, a number of general implications are evident. They are asymmetric because they involve one stationary and one mobile partner. There is a continuum from specialization to generalization in plant–insect relationships, cheating is widespread, especially among insects, and plant–insect mutualism has been dynamic over time, arising and being lost repeatedly. Birds, of course, are also involved in mutualistic pollinating relationships with plants. "Evolutionary theory has a potentially important, but as yet largely unfulfilled, role to play in explaining the origins, maintenance, breakdown and evolution of insect-plant mutualisms," conclude Bronstein and colleagues (2006: 1). We take these relationships for granted, yet without them ecosystems would collapse. We already see crises in many agricultural areas caused by declining insect populations, probably damaged by extensive agricultural use of insecticides, herbicides, and fungicides around the world. Drastic die-offs of bees are increasingly problematic and perhaps the best known, affecting crops from almonds to peaches, as well as wild plants, in ways that have not been adequately studied (Wagner et al. 2021; Potts et al. 2010). Important bird pollinators, with commonly known examples such as hummingbirds in the Americas and honeyeaters in Australia, are also in decline because of environmental poisons, loss of habitat, and climate change.

The evolutionary dance between plants and pollinators must have involved play among a number of semiotic elements, including odors as signals of potential nourishment, touch stimulating reciprocal behaviors between the partners, and visual signals leading to the development of complementary forms. Adolf Portmann (1967) emphasized the central importance of outward form and appearance in animals responding to evolutionary pressures and values. In *Animal Forms and Patterns*, he called attention to the dramatic contrasts between the asymmetrical forms and placements of internal organs, which are often very difficult to distinguish among mammals, for example, and the remarkably differing and symmetrical external appearances of such closely related animals as lions, tigers, and panthers (25–35, 141). "We must assume," he says of the outward appearances of mammals, insects, and fishes, that they have been designed for something more than practical functions of survival, and "that they have also been designed in a very special way to meet the eye of the beholder" (25). We might wish to substitute the active verb "evolved" for the passive construction "been designed for," which Portmann uses, for in the development of mutualistic behaviors among species, reciprocal communication must have gradually resulted in complementary forms and other means of attraction and active cooperation for physical pollination. As Karel Kleisner (2008) remarks of Portmann's original emphasis on the representational aspects of living creatures, "The evolution of particular constituents of the body may be driven, not only by selective pressures that increase their functional utility but also by their ability to interact with the umwelten of other living beings in a meaningful and contextual way" (207).

Early in the twentieth century, Jakob von Uexküll had established the active ways in which organisms select the kinds of interactions they find meaningful in the environments around them; this plays a critical role in their own evolution and that of their mutualistic partners and the environments they share (von Uexküll 1934; Sharov et al. 2015: 361). Fragrances and colors draw pollinators to their hosts, while nectars and the nourishing proteins in pollen are valuable gifts chosen by insects and birds. But the visual appearance of forms must also have been centrally important, so that mimicry is the activity that creates complementary forms like the dramatic one of the hawkmoth and the Madagascar orchid, or the bill of the hummingbird and the long tubular flowers that hold the large amounts of nectar it prefers. Such flowers are beebalms, columbines, daylilies and lupines, foxgloves and hollyhocks. These plants have coevolved such nectaries to attract the birds whose bills can stimulate their reproductive parts and avoid the attentions of other birds or insects. The flower "persuades" the appropriate pollinator to behave as a sexual partner/participate in an erotic dance or conjunction. Some orchids lure pollinators by mimicking the appearance of a female insect so that males of the same species will copulate with the flower. Other types of pollination are not obviously sexual but related to the fragrance of food that draws the pollinator, which in turn performs the movement of pollen from flower to flower. One example is night-blooming flowers that attract bats with strong musty odors.[7]

Pollination is only one example of the many forms of mimicry among plants and animals that have evolved through millions of years of mutualistic communication and interaction. For example, some butterflies and moths have "eyes" on their wings, preying mantises look like thin green or brown sticks, and some caterpillar stages of moths or butterflies (e.g. *Hemeroplanes triptolemus* moth or *Deilephila porcellus* butterfly) can look like sticks but take on the uncanny appearance and movements of snakes in response to a sense of danger (De Bona et al. 2015; see also "Caterpillar Mimics Snake" 2016). Portmann (1967) describes many other examples, such as a cuttlefish that can change its appearance to blend with the seabed where it rests, or waving underwater grasses (192–195). In characterizing Portmann's discussion of mimicry in *Animal*

---

[7]   See www.fs.fed.us/wildflowers/pollinators/What_is_Pollination/syndromes.shtml.

Forms and Patterns [*Die Tiergestalt*], Merleau-Ponty (2003) spoke in his Nature lectures about "an internal relation of resemblance between animal morphology and the milieu. Everything happens as if there were an indivision, a perceptual relation between the two." In the specular relation between animals, "each is a mirror of the other . . . What exists are not separated animals, but an inter-animality" (188–189). Thus mimicry performs an internal knowledge of other animal forms and behaviors gained by long observation and interrelationships, in some cases for mutual benefits for each species, but in others as a way of deceiving predators. There must have developed an internal sense of its function so that the mimicking animal can behave properly for the deception to work. It is an active, complex kind of communication based on a historical sense (memory) of relationship and intersubjectivity, whether for positive gain as in pollination, or in a deceptive purpose of defense (see Maran 2015: 211–212).

Timo Maran describes the long tradition of biological research on mimicry from the nineteenth century to the present but focuses attention on the active semiotic dimensions of meaningful messaging and the "semiotic scaffolding" in Jesper Hoffmeyer's formulation that acts as a formal bodily memory system to shape the mirroring that develops over time. Different organisms "are bound together through perception, recognition, communication and action," explains Maran, "and they act in these relations as subjects, interpreting each-others' perceivable appearances in a species-specific manner while also including their individual ontogenetic experience" (Maran 2015: 212). Hoffmeyer (2015) describes the evolutionary significance of the web of semiotic scaffolding that coordinates the millions, even trillions, of cells in each organism that must somehow recapitulate its own history as it grows from embryo to adult. "Throughout evolution new scaffoldings have been built on top of those already operative. Evolution is primarily about the establishment of successful semiotic scaffolding devices, and genetic mutations are just elementary tools in this process that may often not rely on modifications at the genetic level at all" (250–251). Genes are only semiotic modulators, whereas overall agency and control lie within the cell, the tissue, and the whole organism (Hoffmeyer 2015; see also Noble 2017: 64–65, 145, 171, 220–221; Wheeler 2016: 155).

By now we should notice that the fog of taboo is beginning to lift from around Lamarck's theory of the heritability of acquired characteristics. Denis Noble (2017) explains how Conrad Waddington's experiments with fruit flies in the 1950s already showed how existing organismic plasticity "could be exploited to enable a *particular* acquired characteristic *in response to an environmental change* to be inherited and become assimilated into the genome. To repeat: the characteristic was acquired as a result of an environmental change, and it was inherited" (217). Noble goes on to discuss recent work in epigenetics showing that mechanisms outside the genome (e.g. Ribonucleic acid – RNAs) can also influence inherited traits and are intricately connected to modify an organism. Together with evolutionary developmental biology (evo-devo theory), niche construction and evolvability enable organisms to speed up genetic variation in response to environmental influences. These and other related functions interact with natural selection and internal genetic engineering to enable organisms to evolve, sometimes very quickly. A new synthesis in evolutionary biology is shifting toward systems approaches (Noble 2017: 217, 220–221, 230–231, 235, 245).

In describing Arnold Gesell's and George Coghill's embryological work and Konrad Lorenz's research on instinct, Merleau-Ponty (2003) explained that both emerging fetal forms in humans and in reptiles, and early fragmentary behaviors of young birds, anticipate environments and situations the new animal will face in the future, based on the species' past experience (140–151, 191–193). As Wendy Wheeler (2016) phrased this phenomenon, creatures "expect the earth" they grow into, bearing in the sedimented memory of their internal webs of semiotic scaffolding a project that will shape their adaptations to the whole of life ahead (212–213, 245). Mimicry is central to this process in the evolution of human culture, as we shall see (Section 2, "From *Homo Heidelbergensis* to *Homo Neanderthalensis*").

Like all other creatures, our species evolved in webs of interspecies relationships and interactions with the world around us. The Earth itself scaffolds the deep history of life-forms from the beginning, as layers of sediments laid down, exploded up from the deep core, washed over by floods and rising seas, and uplifted in the movements of the crust literally preserve material remains of past events and life-forms from 3.5 billion years ago. Like the layers of geological deposits, therefore, the sedimentation of meaningful forms in living beings is a kind of material memory that supports behavior, which Hoffmeyer defined as semiotic scaffolding. It is also paralleled by the sedimented structure of the brain, with the most primitive layers at the lowest level atop the spinal cord and later formations above, topped by the cerebrum where our conscious thought is located. As in the rest of our body, all the parts of the brain are communicating with each other continually, so that primitive emotional responses in the limbic system and "reptilian brain" influence and are interrelated with conscious awareness and motor systems (see Coolidge and Wynn 2018: 8–33).

2 Hominin Emergence

Let us now turn to the evidence, which has grown dramatically in the past several decades, of when our kind of animal began to emerge within the rich tangle of mammalian life. In his Nature lectures, Merleau-Ponty quoted Teilhard de Chardin as saying, "Man came silently into the world" (Merleau-Ponty 2003: 267; Chardin 1975: 184.). Assuming this is so, Merleau-Ponty (2003) asks where human consciousness truly appears, explaining that "We do not see [man] any more than we see the moment when consciousness appears in ontogenesis. . . . That the human entered silently also means: no rupture. . . . There is a 'metamorphosis,' not a beginning from zero" (267–268). Paleontologists in Kenya, Ethiopia, Tanzania, and South Africa have since amply confirmed that gradual metamorphosis among coexisting primate species evolved in the direction of the group called "hominini," and then our own *Homo* line, more gradually than was known in the mid-twentieth century when Teilhard and Merleau-Ponty were writing. In the 1950s, Louis and Mary Leakey began discovering evidence of many early apes and hominins in the Olduvai Gorge of Tanzania, with the most famous being Mary's find in 1959 of a complete *Paranthropus boisei* skull. Their son Richard, his wife Maeve, and skilled Kenyan members of their teams, especially Kamoya Kimeu, have since made multiple discoveries of early hominins in Kenya's Rift Valley. Other paleontologists in Ethiopia and South Africa have also found such early hominins (Leakey 2020: 45–222; Haile-Selassie et al. 2019; Dennell 2009: 13–34; Leakey 1994; Leakey 1979; Leakey 1974).

Thus, rather than a clear descent from one ancestor like the famous *Australopithicus* Lucy in the description Teilhard de Chardin provided, paleontologists now see that there were many other similar hominins coexisting at the time of climate changes that increased glaciation in the late Miocene, between seven and five million years ago, which gradually dried out the African plains, sending many apelike creatures out of the trees and onto the ground to find food. The landscape of East Africa was transformed by the reduction of forest cover into flood plain savannas, with woodlands along the rivers. Glaciation advanced in the northern hemisphere and in Antarctica. Apes that had been widespread in Eurasia disappeared with other forest mammals. This was part of a massive faunal turnover caused by dramatic global cooling. Rich troves of hominin fossils from many areas now demonstrate the contemporaneous existence of multiple species of early human ancestors, from *Paranthropus* and *Australopithecus afarensis* to *Homo habilis* and *Homo erectus*. The archaeological record supports this climate picture, with ice cores, deep seabed cores, ancient DNA studies, and faunal records adding crucial evidence.

As grasslands expanded in Africa four million years ago, a semibipedal primate called *Australopithecus anamensis* emerged with both apelike and primitive human features (DeSilva 2021: 74–76; Leakey 2020: 100–101, 130–131, 267; Dennell 2009: 13–19). The first discovery to be widely reported was the famous Lucy in 1974, initially considered a new species – a bipedal link between apes and humans. But earlier, in 1924, Raymond Dart had found another such fossil in South Africa, and before long in the 1970s and 1980s many other similar hominin fossils were unearthed. They seem to have been widely spread around Africa and a number are likely to have coexisted for thousands or even millions of years, as the rough list below suggests (see Leakey 2020: 130–139, 155–156, 171–183; Dennell 2009: 12–19).

Hominin line split from apes, c. six million years ago (mya):

- *Sahelanthropos tchadensis* (Chad – Michel Brunet), possibly 6.8–7.2 mya, but controversial.
- *Ardipithicus kadabba* (Ethiopia – Yohannes Haile-Selassie), 5.8–5.6 mya.
- *Orrorin tugensis* (Kenya), similar age to *kadabba*, primitive teeth but bipedal.
- *Ardipithicus ramidus* (Ethiopia – Tim White), 4.4 mya.
- *Australopithecus anamensis* (Kenya – Maeve Leakey, Ethiopia – Yohannes Haile-Selassie), 3.9–3.6 mya.
- *Australopithecus afarensis* (the famous "Lucy" Hadar, Ethiopia – Don Johanson), 3.2 mya. Both bipedal and arboreal. But preceded by the Tuang Child found by Raymond Dart in South Africa in 1924, 2.8 mya.
- *Astralopithecus sediba* (South Africa – Lee Berger), 1.98 mya.
- *Paranthropus boisei* (Turkana Basin, Kenya – Mary and Louis Leakey), 2.8 mya. Many examples found, coexisting with *Homo erectus*.
- *Paranthropus robustus* (South Africa), 2–1 mya.
- *Homo habilis* (Kenya), c. 2.4 million years ago, or perhaps even older at 2.8 (Leakey 2020: 221).
- *Homo erectus* (Kenya 2 – 1.9 million years ago Richard Leakey, Maeve Leakey, Kamoya Kimeu, and others). The Turkana Boy (or Narioktome specimen) is a key example, whose almost complete skeleton was found by Kamoya Kimeu and dated c. 1.53 million years ago, and who died at about the age of nine years old (Leakey 2020: 230–236).
- *Homo ergaster* (Dmnisi, China, Indonesia), 1.8–1.6 million years ago, perhaps the same as *Homo erectus* but found in Asia; recent find in China of stone tools 2.1 million years old (Zhu et al. 2018).
- *Homo naledi* (South Africa, Lee Berger), 335,000–236,000 years ago.
- *Homo floresiensis* (Island of Flores, Indonesia), so-called Hobbit, living there from 100,000–60,000 years ago and thus overlapping with *Homo erectus*, *Homo neanderthalis*, and *Homo sapiens*.

Dates and places in this list demonstrate the coexistence of some or many of these developing types of hominin and the eventual appearance of the likely ancestor of our own species – *Homo erectus*, the first fully bipedal hominin of our general type – about two million years ago. This ancestor emerged from at least two million years of gradually developing bipedalism and increasingly sophisticated stone tool use that required complex thought (Leakey 2020: 269–271).

Homo Erectus, Climate Change, and Cultural Emergence

Paleontologist Elisabeth Vrba introduced the turnover-pulse hypothesis, which claims that periods of sharp climate change and resulting ecological stress cause rapid extinctions and a high turnover of new species across many lineages (Vrba et al. 1995). Such changes have been caused by variations in the Earth's orbit and magnetic fields, called Milankovitch Cycles (Leakey 2020: 256–267; Rabett 2012: 10–12). These are tilts in the Earth's axis (obliquity), variations in its orbit around the sun from circular to elliptical (eccentricity), and a wobble in orbit caused by the gravity of sun and moon and the bulge at the Earth's equator (precession). Fossil evidence has been found for three marked drying periods and peaks in faunal richness and species turnover in East Africa: 3.8–3.3, 2.8–2.4, and 2–1.8 million years ago (Leakey 2020: 194, 268–270; see also Bobe and Behrensmeyer 2004). Maeve Leakey (2020) explains that during the last 800,000 years at least eighteen separate glacial advances and retreats have occurred at approximately 100,000 year intervals under the influence of the eccentricity cycle. "On the grand scale, this is the icehouse world that *Homo erectus* evolved in, and it must surely have played a huge role in shaping our ancestor's evolution" (268).

Bipedalism

The coexistence of various kinds of hominins during this period is a critical reality that changes how we can think of the tangled inheritance that produced us. What did all these walking apes have in common? The early stages of their gradual movement from arboreal existence into bipedal foraging on the ground were full of danger from violent predation in open spaces.[8] Foraging initially took place on forest edges, with return to the trees for sleep and safety from saber-toothed tigers, large and ferocious animals similar to a wolverine, and huge hyenas or crocodiles (DeSilva 2021:77; Leakey 2020: 109). A tibia found at Kanapoi gives clear evidence of bipedalism as far back as 4.2 million years ago (Leakey 2020: 129–130, 139).

The first dramatic evidence of fully functional bipedalism was the famous 3.6 million-year-old Laetoli footprints found by Mary Leakey in 1978. In a layer

---

[8] In fact, a new hypothesis by Dartmouth paleoanthropologist Jeremy DeSilva (2021) suggests that bipedalism may have been common among apes in Europe before climate change caused their disappearance, and thus may have preceded the emergence of hominins (79–86).

of fossilized volcanic ash, the prints of many animals including rhinos, giraffes, baboons, gazelles, an early type of elephant, and buffalos were accompanied by the footprints of three hominins – two adults and a smaller individual. The excavated trail was more than twenty-seven meters long (88 feet), so that foot structure and gait were clearly indicated. The prints were made by early representatives of *Australopithecus afarensis*, a capable walker with heel strikes and strides much like ours; but these hominins were also arboreal, needing the safety of trees to avoid predators and for sleeping (De Silva 2021: 93–100; Leakey 2020: 134–136). They were probably omnivorous, eating fruits, seeds, and nuts in the trees, and termites, grubs, eggs, reptiles, and small mammals on the ground (Dennell 2009: 17).

Bipedalism wrought huge changes in behavior and physical development, but not immediately. Until recently, bipedalism was thought to have rather quickly enabled the growth of larger brains as well as manual dexterity and sophisticated toolmaking. "We have since learned," says Maeve Leakey (2020), "that brain enlargement was an attribute acquired quite late in human evolution as a result of other adaptations made possible by the move to bipedality" (214). Indeed, it took more than a million years for the brain of early hominins to enlarge to the size of that of *Homo erectus*, which, at around 800 cm, is 50 percent larger than that of an *Australopithecus* and halfway between that of a chimpanzee (384 cm) and a modern adult human (1,300 cm) (Leakey 2020: 232–234; DeSilva 2021: 109). But during the long period of *Homo erectus'* flourishing and migration across the globe, brain size increased to 1,000 cm as new environments and challenges and cultural development spurred enlargement (Van Arsdale 2013).

Terrence Deacon has asserted that "hominids' behavioral adaptations have determined the course of their physical evolution, rather than vice versa," with the development of increasingly sophisticated stone tools as "behavioral prostheses for obtaining food and organizing social behaviors [becoming] indispensable elements in a new adaptive complex" (Deacon 1997: 345). The cultural transmission of toolmaking techniques and strategies for hunting and foraging were symbolic behaviors that allowed increasingly successful adaptations to environmental changes and also led to physical changes such as "loss of sexual dimorphism, more efficient bipedalism, more complete precision grip, and increased brain size ... Ultimately, all these curious physical traits that distinguish modern human bodies and brains were caused by *ideas* shared down generations" (Deacon 1997: 349). Deacon's view of hominin evolution is distinctively focused on the symbolic cognitive processes which he believes allowed increased flexibility in a coevolutionary network that included the development of language and representational functions which become apparent when Neanderthals and anatomically modern humans appear, as we shall see.

Environment Shapes Culture

At this point we should emphasize how hominin behavior and culture were shaped by adaptations to changing environments; these, in turn, also affected the spaces and ecological relationships around them. Noble (2017) reminds us that a central characteristic of living processes "is their sensitivity to the logic of their context" and the ways that the networks of interactions in the environment shape them just as the networks within the organisms do (258). Lewontin (2000) echoes Uexküll's focus on each organism's particular agency as dependent on what kinds of stimuli it has evolved to register: "organisms not only determine what aspects of the outside world are relevant to them by peculiarities of their shape and metabolism but they actively construct, in the literal sense of the word, a world around themselves" (54–55). Birds make nests, crabs and oysters make shells, ants and termites create mounds, beavers shape whole watery landscapes with their dams and lodges. "In fact," Lewontin says, "all terrestrial organisms, both plants and animals, create shells around themselves that can be observed with simple instrumentation" (54). Special cameras can capture images of the layers of warm air around a human body, for example, that protect it from the surrounding atmosphere. Plants similarly create atmospheric layers around themselves and exude moisture at night. Just as important, Lewontin (2000) explains, living plants, animals, birds, and insects "are in a constant process of altering their environment" and "every act of consumption is also an act of production" as living systems transform materials by consuming them and excreting matter and energy in other forms (54–55; see also Odling-Smee et al. 2003). According to Alexei Sharov, Timo Maran, and Morten Tønnessen (2015), organisms can reshape sign relations regarding environmental cues and resources, thus manipulating to some degree the ecological situations around them. Interactions and communication between species are important factors in community survival and can lead to species change and the emergence of new species (362).

Hominins were integrally enmeshed within coevolving ecosystems of plants and animals, adapting with them as climate and geography changed, especially during stressful periods like the vast faunal extinction event and following surge of new species between seven and five million years ago (DeSilva 2021; Leakey 2020: 80–88, 267, 276; Dennell 2009). During that period, as we have seen, the climate cooled dramatically, and developing glaciation in the far northern and southern areas dried out vast stretches of Africa and Asia. Sea levels dropped as glaciation captured enormous amounts of moisture, so that the sea was about 120 meters lower than at present. Many animals had to learn to exist on new food sources such as harsh grasses rather than tender foliage as forested areas shrank (Leakey 2020; Dennell 2009). These adaptations required many kinds of mutualism, with animals responding to each other and also affecting the distribution of plants when creating niches for survival at the same time that grassland plants were colonizing areas that had previously been wetter and forested. Plants seem to have been active participants in gradual processes of domestication, rather than only passive subjects of human manipulation. So plant–hominin coevolution as far back as the Pliocene resulted in broad plant communities adapting to human changes in the environment around them (Allaby et al. 2014). We can only struggle to imagine what those interrelations might have been in more specific terms. Perhaps the effects the Australian landscape and its first human arrivals had upon each other can serve as a partial example, as Bruce Pascoe (2018) explains.

The patterns of behavior that evolved with these changes can be associated with the emergence of hominin cultures of sophisticated lithic technologies, cooperative hunting strategies, migration planning and movements across new ecosystems, the gradually developing ability to control fire, and the development of clothing and other domestic material arrangements. For our purposes, culture will be defined as those patterned actions and their material objects and results that shape life processes, organize social behaviors, and solidify affective relationships between members of the same species. This general concept provides a working definition that can be the premise for suggesting elements in the evolution of culture from *Australopithecines* to *Homo erectus* and eventually to *Homo sapiens*. Peter Richerson emphasizes the communicative aspects of culture as "all of the information that individuals acquire from others by a variety of social learning processes including teaching and imitation. Transmission fidelity is often sufficiently high for culture to act as an inheritance system" (Richerson et al. 2010: 8985–8986).

Thus culture provides semiotic scaffolding in Hoffmeyer's, Sharov's, and Maran's terms, even if verbal language is not involved. Similar patterns are noticeable across many animal groups such as monkeys, apes, beavers, dogs, birds, and whales. Impalas flee at the alarm calls of wild dogs, for example; vervet monkeys have "words" for leopard, eagle, snake, baboon, and rival troops that other creatures around them respond to; chimpanzees use scores of different call combinations; dolphins and whales communicate with far-reaching songs (Safina 2015: 86–92). Culture is therefore a continuum of organized behaviors in animals, and hominin cultural development emerges from gradual adaptations in the dynamic lives of our ancestors as climates changed and technologies and social patterns coevolved with their environments. Increasing brain size accompanied emerging practices including the increased eating of meat, hunting, increasing use and sophistication of stone tools, the use of fire, and the adoption of clothing. Genetic changes accompanied these cultural innovations over time, forming the scaffolding that would support further adaptations to new climates, landscapes, and environments as climate continued to change and hominins moved around Africa and eventually migrated beyond (Sharov et al. 2015; Richerson et al. 2010).

Homo Erectus and Meat

Evidence for occasional meat-eating appears very early in *Australopithecus*, with the robust lineage having large teeth indicating a feeding niche of tough, fibrous vegetation, while more gracile lines had smaller molars and probably ate softer foods such as fruits, seeds, insects, and some small creatures like lizards (Leakey 2020: 220). As early as 3.4 million years ago, they were able to scavenge meat from kills of large predators by using sharp rocks (DeSilva 2021: 102–103). But Maeve Leakey (2020) says that by the time *Homo erectus* appeared, "a strategy for securing meat with relative ease and safety had been adopted" (243). Archaeological remains at the Turkana site in Kenya, where Leakey's team worked, contain the bones of a type of elephant, a species of giraffe, monkeys, rodents, zebras, rhinos, hippos, pigs, and antelopes. Along with these animals, *Homo erectus* also ate reptiles and birds and must have eaten many insects, eggs, and crustaceans (270). Such a rich and varied diet of meat was linked to shrinking intestinal size because less space was needed for digesting plant materials. This higher density nourishment enabled the development of a larger brain and was driven by a drying habitat that lacked easy access to fruits and vegetation. All these factors affected each other as *Homo erectus* evolved.

These hominins had to search large areas to find prey and they had to compete with specialist carnivores like saber-toothed cats and hyenas. They seem to have succeeded because those predators became extinct in Africa around the time *Homo erectus* became prominent (Leakey 2020: 244). Hunting techniques would have required close knowledge of prey, thus a kind of coexistence side by side of the kind still seen in the wild animals of Kenya and Tanzania – for example, Ngorongoro Crater lions, hyenas, cheetahs, and wild dogs who live alongside herds of wildebeest, zebras, and gazelles, moving along the periphery of their herds, occasionally choosing one animal to chase down and kill. These animals practice a complex kind of mutualism and interrelationship, fully aware of each other's presence and sharing the same water holes, though at different times. Maeve Leakey suggests that *Homo erectus* became even more efficient at hunting than other carnivores by using a kind of "persistence running" similar to present-day marathon runners. The ability to run at a moderate speed for long distances and track animals as they sought to escape would tire gazelles and larger grazing animals like kudu or zebras that can only run at high speed for short distances. This persistence hunting strategy is still practiced by traditional societies such as the Bushmen of the Kalahari, the Tarahumara of northern Mexico, the Navajo and Paiutes of the American Southwest, and Australian aborigines. Social networking, complex cooperation, and intimate knowledge of animal behaviors and terrain is required for such hunting, as are planning the hunt and tracking skills that have to be passed on from generation to generation (Leakey 2020: 245–249; Bramble and Lieberman 2004).

The use of complex stone tools preceded the appearance of the *Homo* lineage, with the earliest known so far to have been dated at 3.3 million years old. These show clear evidence that their makers had significant manual dexterity and technical understanding of stone types and the ways stones can be fractured. Tools were made from preselected cores that were then struck with sophisticated skills to produce sharp flakes. Such skills must have resulted from the transmission of traditional knowledge between generations and also probably from imitation as their makers learned from elders (Leakey 2020: 191). Relatively crude Oldowan hand axes, scrapers, and sharp flakes were used by early *Homo erectus,* but later in this hominin's evolution – by 1.5 million years ago – tools became more precise, finely shaped biface tools with long, sharp edges, both hand axes and cleavers. They seem to have been carried from place to place and used for many purposes from butchering to scraping hides, to working wood (Coolidge and Wynn 2018: 121–124). These more sophisticated tools are classified as Acheulean and found both at Olduvai and in South Asian sites where *Homo erectus* had migrated from Africa (Van Arsdale 2013; Dennell 2009: 103). Some stone cores and tools show the effects of heating with fire to improve working quality (Alperson-Afil 2017; Gowlett 2016; Peris et al. 2012).

The use of fire was a key accomplishment that allowed *Homo erectus* to process food, provide heat, and eventually shape environments. Many animals benefit from opportunistic association with wildfires; they capture animals seeking to escape from the flames and find accidentally cooked bodies of those who died in fires. Various raptors are known to be drawn to prairie fires for this purpose, and some birds even intentionally spread fires themselves (Ackerman 2020: 220; Bonta et al. 2017; Barnard 1987). "Fire foraging" in this way probably led early hominins to discover roots, eggs, and meat that had been accidentally cooked, as they mimicked the ways other animals benefited from proximity to fire. By the time of *Homo erectus*, at least a million years ago, the use of fire seems to have become deliberate and controlled. Evidence of the use of fire-prepared adhesives dates from a half million years ago, and actual hearths appear in the archaeological record dating from at least 300,000 years ago and probably earlier. The increased height and brain size of *Homo erectus* over its Australopithecine predecessors may be related to the wider and more digestible diet made possible by cooked tubers and other vegetation as well as meat (Gowlett 2016: 3–7). These developments represent complex cultural as well as technological changes, because the use of fire required group cooperation and the learning of skills that became shared behavioral habits and created social bonding. Fires became centers of social activity, including sheltering, toolmaking, and cooking.

The benefits of fire can mitigate some of the effects of cold climate, but fire can only provide temporary relief when groups are resting in one place. The daytime life of *Homo erectus* was one of active foraging and hunting out in open grasslands, exposed to the weather which cooled and dried, as we have seen. Were they naked, or did they have clothes? Archaeological remains from periods as far back as two or even one million years ago do not include organic materials that might have been used to protect the body from cold, because animal skins or textiles made from plants degrade too quickly. Ian Gilligan draws together archaeological evidence that could indirectly suggest the fashioning of clothing, first simple cloaks for early *Homo* species, and later complex clothing that fit closely around the body as a more effective protective layer to retain body heat. He speculates that archaic hominins probably lost their fur before the beginning of the Pleistocene and explains that we remain a tropical species that can tolerate heat better than cold. When the ice age began and climate in Africa cooled and dried, our ancestors had to find ways to survive. More was needed than fire; animal skins must have been used very early. Stone scraping tools are found in Olduvai deposits, suggesting that animal hides were scraped regularly. This kind of tool becomes more precise and sharp with the development of Acheulean tool kits, and scraper tools are found to be more and more prevalent in middle latitudes where colder temperatures were typical. Thus, our *Homo erectus* ancestors must have had simple cloaks made from animal hides for protection as they moved out of Africa and began to spread north and east. Complex clothing requiring sewing would come later and be indicated by the presence of bone awls and eyed needles in archaeological remains from as early as 40,000 years ago in northern China and Western Europe (Gilligan 2018: 36–37, 47–55, 76–82).

Homo erectus was a remarkably successful migrant, moving out of Africa probably through grasslands along the Nile and then into Asia along the Sinai Peninsula and the Levant, or across the southern end of the Red Sea during brief warmer and wetter periods between colder spells. Its fossilized remains are found in Dminisi, in the Caucasus mountains of Georgia dating to 1.8 million years ago and in Ubeidiya, Israel with an age about 1.4 million years ago. As early as 1.6 million years ago it had reached the area of Bejing, and by 1.6 million years ago *Homo erectus* was living in Java, where it lasted until some point between 117,000 and 108,000 (Leakey 2020: 275–279; Rizal et al. 2020).

Why did this talented hominin leave its African homeland? How did it manage? It is quite likely that *erectus* was following the herds and flocks of its fellow animals, as they all sought better climates and landscapes to support their needs. Hominins would have moved with the whole faunal and plant community as the climate fluctuated . "In warm, moist interglacial periods, faunal and botanical communities would have expanded northwards and often longitudinally, but contracted southwards during cold, dry glacial periods," says Robin Dennell (2009: 199). If he is correct, the migrations of *Homo erectus* would have been episodic and spatially discontinuous, with the periods of cool and dry climate alternating with warmer and wetter periods. During cooler times, migrants would likely have stayed in relatively sheltered landscapes such as the Levant, western Turkey, and sheltered parts of the Caucasus mountains (Leakey 2020: 277–281; Dennell 2009: 201–202; Finlayson 2004: 41–42, 50).[9]

Homo erectus thus emerged during particularly extreme climate variations and managed to flourish and rapidly spread across Eurasia for almost two million years during these intense environmental upheavals. Its travels included crossing mountains and rivers, and even short ocean passages between the Asian continent and the Indonesian islands. These ancient ancestors not only had to travel in bands that were cohesive and engaged in planning and cooperative adaptations, they had to hunt and cook foods that included new kinds of vegetation and therefore must have been able to communicate in some sort of protolanguage (Leakey 2020: 248–249).[10] Perhaps most amazingly, they must have used watercraft of some kind, because their migratory paths included large rivers such as the Euphrates, the Indus, and the Ganges. Even if the sea was 120 meters (360 feet) lower than at present, there could still have been open water to cross from what is now Thailand, Cambodia, Vietnam, and Malaysia to reach a long chain of Indonesian islands (Leakey 2020; Rabett 2012: 57; Dennell 2009; Finlayson 2004: 41).

---

[9] Dennell entertains the possibility that *Homo erectus* could have developed in Southwest Asia and then dispersed back into Africa because of the primitive qualities of the Dminisi specimens, but he accepts the consensus that hominins, including the genus *Homo*, probably originated in Africa.

[10] Intriguing evidence for the gestural origins of language was recently published by an international group of researchers led by Nicolas Fay (Fay et al. 2022), though of course the issue remains much debated.

At this point let us summarize the importance of *Homo erectus* and its long flourishing as our ancestry developed along a separate path from other primates. This energetic hominin had a flat face and much smaller teeth compared to *Australopithicus* and other preceding and contemporary ground-dwelling kindred. Its body was taller and slimmer (around five feet tall, on average, for adults), lacking body hair, and fully bipedal and erect in its stance, much like modern humans. *Homo erectus* also diverged from earlier types in lacking sexual dimorphism, or dramatic size differences between males and females. During the long span of its existence, brain size increased along with meat-eating and complex manual dexterity and skills from around 800 cm in early specimens to 1,000 cm in late *erectus* examples, thus approaching the 1,300 cm norm for modern humans.

Cultural development accompanied these changes, building on the scaffolding of behaviors established among other apelike ancestors. Long-existing tendencies of sociability had become complex habits of cooperation and communication based on some kind of protolanguage that made intimate knowledge of landscapes and food sources transmissible. Such knowledge enabled planning and ecological adaptability and supported increasingly skilled stone Achulean toolmaking, the use of fire, and effective hunting strategies. A diverse diet including plants, but especially reliant on meat, was necessarily involved in the gradual expansion of brain size. Boldness and enterprise must have been characteristic of *Homo erectus* as it grew more successful, and such traits led groups of these hominins to venture, in waves, farther and farther away from their original African home. This remarkable geographical expansion took *Homo erectus* up the Nile valley and into the Levant in only a few hundred thousand years during periods of warmer and wetter climate that temporarily turned the Sahara and parts of the Arabian peninsula into grasslands, attracting migrating faunal populations of many kinds. Within another 200,000 years after establishing themselves in what are now Israel and Jordan, and across Turkey to the Caucasus Mountians, they had reached as far as Northern China and the Indonesian Islands where they remained until disappearing a little more than 100,000 years ago when Neanderthals were already wandering throughout western Eurasia.

From this point onward, our focus will be primarily European and West Asian, because most paleontological research has occurred there, and we look at the beginnings of cultures most directly ancestral to our own. According to Robin Dennell (2009), Chinese archaeology is not very fully developed; he says that "the early Paleolithic potential of this vast country has scarcely been tapped," although he predicts spectacular discoveries in the coming decade (166). His book *The Paleolithic Settlement of Asia* provides a richly detailed summary of what is known at present.

From *Homo Heidelbergensis* to *Homo Neanderthalensis*

From the remarkable *Homo erectus*, even more skilled and capable hominins evolved, so that by 700,000 years ago or so their descendants were living in northern Europe during interglacial periods, until around 400,000 years ago. They were named *Homo heidelbergensis*, after the 1908 discovery of a fossilized jaw in a sandpit near Heidelberg, Germany. Since then the term has been generalized to cover remains found in eastern England, Spain, and Italy, as well as in Germany, Israel, and parts of Africa.[11] They are characterized by a larger brain size averaging 1,230 cm and a higher and more rounded cranium than *Homo erectus*. This is not yet a fully modern skull shape, but it has larger frontoparietal areas associated with manipulation of objects and precise gestures (specifically active in stone-knapping) that may be related to the development of language. Frederick Coolidge and Thomas Wynn (2018) believe that the beginnings of modern thinking developed during the time of this hominin. They conclude that both syntax and the use of symbols are involved here with increasingly sophisticated tool use, social interaction, and communication (159, 187).

Building upon the cultural scaffolding of *Homo erectus*' predecessors, *Homo heidelbergensis* continued to refine Acheulean lithic technology. They made increasingly symmetrical, often finely shaped, thin hand axes and blades, some heat-tempered and finished with bone tools. The finest of these tools display clearly aesthetic qualities. To make them, individuals carried specially selected cores with them and struck off flints and blades for specific purposes when needed. This process is known from the reconstruction of cores by archaeologists at knapping sites where the pieces are all found together. Boxgrove on the coast of southeastern England offered such a site where cliff erosion has exposed groups of stone tools from 500,000 years ago. These deposits represent a short time period of 20–100 years and the deliberate use of space by individual knappers who used rough hand axes as cores for making flakes to use in butchering. One such site was focused on the butchery of a horse and another was a freshwater pond around which were found dense patches of flakes and the bones of many butchered animals. Formation of three-dimensional, symmetrical biface tools,

---

[11] Some debate continues about the identity of all the archaic hominins found in Europe, so that some archaeologists prefer to classify particular European remains as *Homo antecessor* or *Homo cepanensis*, and still other terms for African specimens. However, most researchers agree on the more general term, as Robin Dennell (2009) explains (454-460). See also M. G. Leakey (2020: 306–307).

especially the finer ones, required cognitive abilities to imagine space that were not used by their *Homo erectus* ancestor. The knapper had to project images of the desired object from a variety of perspectives not visible simultaneously, and shape the hand axe accordingly, from an imagined geometrical ideal form that guided their actions (Coolidge and Wynn 2018: 171–176; Cunliffe 2012: 43). Such cognitive abilities were surely only part of a wider intellectual capacity for imagining spaces in the landscape, projecting travel routes in familiar areas, and indeed understanding time sequences in many of their activities, the movements of other animals, and in the passage of seasons and weather systems.

These archaic humans used fire and hunted large game effectively. Likely using natural shelters such as caves, they also may have built wooden structures, according to evidence of post holes found in Terra Amata, France, and they used wooden tools such as spears. Culturally transmitted habits and techniques for making loose cloaks and carrying containers, cords and ropes, and other perishable material objects must have been part of their domestic lives. Like their ancient ancestors, they moved with the herds of animals and changing vegetation as the climate alternately warmed and cooled with glacial advances and retreats up through the Last Glacial Maximum lasting from around 33,000 to 15,000 years ago (Smithsonian National Museum of Human History 2021; Coolidge and Wynn 2018; Dennell 2009). But because the glacial advances during this period were so dramatic and long-lasting, only around 25 percent of these thousands of years were favorable for ancient humans and their larger faunal community in northern Europe. At their extremes, glaciers over a mile (almost 2 km) thick reached down over most of the British Isles and deep into Germany, and from 180,000–70,000 years ago those lands were virtually empty of animal life (Coolidge and Wynn 2018: 162; Cunliffe 2012: 44–45). Such climate changes were some of the most extreme on Earth for many millions of years, and adapting successfully to them must have spurred the cognitive development of hominins so that this transitional stage of several hundred thousand years gave rise to the better-known *Homo neanderthalensis* and its chronological overlap with our own modern kind of human.

Homo neanderthalensis was named after the German valley where fossils were unearthed in a quarry in the middle of the nineteenth century. Since that time many more Neanderthal remains have been found all over Europe, in the Middle East, and as far away as Siberia. Early stereotypes of hairy apelike creatures – the classic cave man with a club – have gradually been replaced by a human cousin with most of the same traits we still have today. Ancient DNA studies, comparative anatomy, increasing numbers of archaeological discoveries, and computer technologies for projecting complete physical images based on skeletal remains have all enabled this greatly revised picture of our nearest hominin cousins. We now know that many had red hair and blue or green eyes, and relatively light skin. DNA studies have revealed that we shared a common ancestor around 500,000 years ago (Reich 2018: 30). Most present humans outside of Africa share 2–4 percent of our genetic makeup with them because of relatively brief periods of interbreeding during several thousand years of coexistence after our modern human ancestors moved out of Africa into the Levant and then into Europe. If we met a Neanderthal man on a city street dressed in a suit, we would not find him monstrous but only a little strange looking with his large nose, shorter brow, and stocky build. The similarities in their appearance, intelligence, and ways of living make it understandable that close, even intimate, encounters between Neanderthals and our kind of human could have occurred. The mystery is their extinction only a few thousand years after our arrival in their homelands (Deacon 1997: 371–373).

In appearance, Neanderthals had compact bodies adapted for the ice age environments around them. They were broader in build, with shorter forearms and lower legs than *Homo sapiens*, a barrel chest, and wider pelvis. Arm bones for both males and females were shaped for heavy musculature and upper body strength. They ranged in height from an average of 5 feet 6 inches in males to 5 feet 1 inch in females, probably not very different from the modern humans that began moving into their territories around 54,000 years ago (Callaway 2022). Their faces were large with heavy brows and their skull shape was somewhat lower and longer than ours. These features are clearly descended from *Homo heidelbergensis* and even resembe *Homo erectus* in some respects. But the striking difference from those ancestors is the large size of their brains, ranging from 1,250–1,700 cubic centimeters, noticeably larger than the modern human brain by about 9 to 13 percent. They seem to have had larger occipital cortices and smaller olfactory bulbs, so that perhaps they would have relied more on visual abilities than smell (Coolidge and Wynn 2018: 191–197). Clearly they inherited and further developed the cognitive abilities of their *heidelbergensis* ancestors.

The greatest number of Neanderthal fossils has come from Western Europe, chiefly Spain, France, and Germany. Populations were small and sparsely located and, like their predecessors, they moved with the faunal communities in response to advances and retreats of ice sheets. It is very important to remember how unstable Pleistocene climates were, fluctuating sometimes very rapidly between very cold periods requiring retreat to southerly refuges and interglacial spells of warmer temperatures allowing a return to areas farther north. In Britain, sometimes almost covered by glaciation, only two Neanderthal sites have been found, thus implying infrequent habitation (Gilligan 2018: 97–102; Walker 2017; Cunliffe 2012: 43–44). Neanderthals survived several hundred thousand years of adaptation to cold and unstable conditions, living and hunting near forests and wearing some kind of animal skin cloaks when conditions became difficult for their cold-adapted bodies and habits (Gilligan 2018: 99–100). They seem to have sheltered in caves, where their bones and temporary hearths have been found, and they had cultural traditions of communal care for injured members, possible occasional burial of the dead, the use of ocre for decoration, and some use of bone tools as well as lithic technologies that included the hafting of stone points on wooden shafts (Papagianni and Morse 2015: loc. 1776–1997).

The shaping of stone tools grew more and more complex from *Homo erectus* and during the thousands of years leading to the emergence of Neanderthals; and the variety of edge types increased with Neanderthal technology whose specialized instruments replaced the multipurpose handaxe (Coolidge and Wynn 2018: 201; see also Leakey 2020: 319–320). Stone tools remained more or less the same for 150,000 years, fashioned with the hallmark *Levallois* techniques of striking an already sharp flake from a core and creating increasingly graceful and symmetrical blades. Such precisely skilled knapping demonstrates forethought, abstract concepts of shape and sequencing, planning for the finished object, and very controlled and delicate striking movements. The whole suite of behaviors was culturally scaffolded from long group experience and beginners had to learn it by closely observing and mimicking expert older teachers during a serious apprenticeship. Neanderthals were apex predators who hunted large mammals at close range, indicated by the many severe skeletal injuries found in upper body remains (Leakey 2020: 316). Their diet was predominately meat, but also included plants, seeds, legumes, roots, mushrooms, and fish for those in coastal areas.

The hunting and foraging activities of Neanderthals required a wide cultural base of traditional knowledge, a long-term semiotic scaffolding built up over thousands of years by their hominin predecessors. More particularly, they built upon the activities and cultural understandings of *Homo heidelbergensis* from whom they descended, shaping their behaviors according to the environmental conditions they experienced. Further east in China, Peking Man, another subspecies of *Homo erectus* had developed and passed down similar behaviors. As Alexander Marshack surmises, this hominin would have had to carefully reckon the seasons of animal migrations and the flowering and fruiting of the plants he relied on for food. "For one thing, *Homo erectus* was omnivorous and had been evolving in that line for millions of years, and to be successfully omnivorous requires a knowledge of the range and potential of the differing sources and resources of each season"

(Marshack 1972: 116). These cultural resources and behaviors were inherited and shared by more modern humans.

Marshack (1972) imagines that the understanding of fire must have been part of this inheritance. Assuming that early human minds were very much like our own, he thinks fire must have seemed to them a living thing.

> It must be tended; it needs a home and place out of the great winds, the heavy rains, the deep snows; it must be constantly fed; it sleeps in embers and can die, yet it can also be blown back to life by the breath; it can burn a hand; it sputters angrily and brightly with animal fat; it dies entirely in water; it whispers, hisses, or crackles, and therefore has a variable 'voice'; it uses itself up, transforming a large weight of wood to gray ash. (113)

People who use fire are involved in complex processes that require forethought, gathering of fuel, "making" fire come to life, and controlling its behavior. Marshack defines these behaviors as an "artificial" ritualized and consciously maintained dramatic realm that was already apparent 500,000 years ago in the charcoal remains of hearths in China and likely to have also been part of the lives of archaic *Homo* predecessors in Africa, whose Neanderthal descendants moved out to colonize Eurasia.

We now know that Neanderthals had language (Conde-Valverde et al. 2021; Imbler 2021; Deacon 1997: 372) and used symbolic decorations of shells and red ochre. Recent discoveries of red ochre and black paintings in three different Spanish caves have been dated to around 65,000 years old, and thus must predate the arrival of *Homo sapiens* in the Iberian Peninsula 20,000 years later, having therefore been produced by Neanderthals (Hoffmann et al. 2018). The caves are in three different Spanish regions: La Pasiega in the north, Ardales in the south, and Maltravieso in the western central region, suggesting widespread practice. The images are patterns of red dots, ladder-like geometric shapes, hand stencils, and hand prints (Hoffmann et al. 2018). This dramatic evidence, together with a few examples of carvings on bone, decorated shells, and possible adornments made of fangs and claws, suggests aesthetic cultural practices and abstract thought. Fairly sparse in comparison with the famous cave art produced by modern humans from 38,000 to 10,000 years ago, Neanderthal remains nevertheless allow a glimpse of cultural qualities approaching, or even overlapping with, those that came after them (see Deacon 1997: 372–373).

The mystery of Neanderthal disappearance has no clear resolution but was likely to have been caused by a combination of challenges that overwhelmed their relatively small population. These include already shrinking numbers before the arrival of modern humans, perhaps caused by the continued stress of increasingly cold events happening too quickly for adaptation. Ian Gilligan explains that there were at least five unusually severe and rapid swings in European climate between 50,000 and 40,000 years ago, just the period when anatomically modern humans were moving into the continent from the Levant. One such cold swing was caused by a Heinrich event that caused large numbers of icebergs to enter the North Atlantic 46,000 years ago and chill northern Europe; another even more abrupt event occurred 40,000 years ago, about the time Neanderthals went extinct. These were periods of especially cold winters and strong winds that could develop in only a decade and would have over-whelmed Neanderthal abilities to move quickly enough to the south to avoid hypothermia (Gilligan 2018: 100–101). The last sites occupied by Neanderthals were caves on Gibraltar, on the southwestern edge of their European range. But the contemporaneous arrival of *Homo sapiens* must have been related to their disappearance. There is no evidence for violent conflict between these groups (Coolidge and Wynn 2018: 233). Instead, it seems that Neanderthals perished by failing at competition for resources with the newcomers who likely had complex clothing to protect them from the cold (Gilligan 2018: 102). The eruption of the Campi Flegrei supervolcano outside of present-day Naples around 39,000 years ago could have made conditions worse as the dust clouds blocked the sun and caused exceedingly harsh winters for several years that seem to have extinguished modern human cultures as dramatically as it did Neanderthals in the same archaeological layer of ash (Reich 2018: 90).

An added twist to the story of hominin interrelations is the discovery of another related species, named Denisovan after the cave in the Siberian Altai where a few of their remains were found in 2008. Only a finger bone and a molar were discovered initially, the bone belonging to a young female and dated somewhere between 76,000 and 51,000 years ago, but DNA sequencing at two different labs (Svante Pääbo's at the Max Planck Institute in Germany and the Lawrence Berkeley National Laboratory in California) showed that it was a different hominin from either Neanderthal or modern human, both of whose remains were also found in the cave but at different chronological levels. This Denisovan DNA was then found to exist in Melanesian, Papuan, and Australian aboriginal populations today, at around 5 percent. At first the evidence for this hominin cousin seemed slim, but later DNA from a hybrid Denisovan/Neanderthal female was found in a fossil in the cave in the Altai and then a 160,000 year old mandible was discovered in a Tibetan cave which also turned out to be Denisovan (Gibbons 2021; Max-Planck Gesselschaft 2019; Slon et al. 2018; Reich 2011). Denisovans had acclimated to the high altitude and low oxygen atmosphere of that area and may have contributed genetic material to later Tibetans that helped them adapt to that environment

(Huerta-Sánchez et al. 2014). The nearly complete skull of "Dragon Man" found in China may also be Denisovan (Gibbons 2021). It now seems clear that at least three kinds of hominins existed at the same time in east Asia and, at least occasionally, interbred. And David Reich announces that ancient DNA evidence from other "ghost humans" indicates that several other archaic hominins must have been present in Asia and contributed still other genomic material to later generations. Reich thinks that some of this evidence may link up with Robin Dennell's view that archaic Eurasian mixtures from *Homo erectus* (or *ergaster)* later returned to Africa and became the basis for the evolution of anatomically modern humans before they migrated out of Africa 70,000 or more years ago (Reich 2018: 67–74).

3 *Homo Sapiens* Appears

Homo sapiens evolved from *Homo erectus* and its descendant *heidelbergensis* (or, as it is also called, *Homo rhodesiensis*) in Africa, in a separate line of descent from Neanderthals, about 500,000 years ago; it began to appear in anatomically modern form around 200,000 years ago. One of the oldest specimens was found in 1967 at Turkana, Kenya, by Kamoya Kimeu – a complete skull and partial skeleton 130,000 years old (Leakey 2020: 305–313). Recently, a very early example was found in Morocco that is 300,000 years old, indicating a gradual development from archaic examples with a flat face like ours but an elongated cranial and brain shape that had yet to develop into the globular form of truly modern humans (Gibbons 2017). Anatomically modern humans seem to have evolved in various regions of Africa before migrating northward along the same routes followed by their archaic ancestors more than a million years before (Leakey 2020: 313; Coolidge and Wynn 2018: 231–233). These anatomically modern humans moved into the Levant around 128,000 years ago when Neanderthals may have already been living there, likely in a warm and wet period. At that time, there was probably not much difference in the behavior and lithic technology of the two archaic humans. They lived side by side for several thousand years, but anatomically modern humans seem to have retreated to Africa as the climate cooled around 75,000 years ago.

When the climate warmed again around 15,000 years later, grasses returned to the Sahara and the Nile Valley and also to western areas of the Arabian Peninsula. *Homo sapiens* once again moved north with the wider faunal community from Africa. It is even possible that some had never retreated from Arabia but instead moved out of the Middle East into Southern India, Sri Lanka, and even Indonesia and Australia. But those modern humans who did return to the Middle East from Africa had complex clothing that allowed continued adaptation to colder spells and movement farther north, west, and east. First evident in the archaeological record from around 75,000 years ago in South Africa, bone awls as well as scrapers and blades suggest that complex, fitted clothing was being created to adapt to the cooler phase of the climate. Toward the end of their existence, Neanderthals also used scrapers, bone tools, and awls, possibly developing complex clothing between 51,000 and 42,000 years ago, but it seems to have been too late to stop the decline in their population. For *Homo sapiens*, however, the advancement of sewing for fitted and layered clothing continued as they moved into colder climates, with eyed needles beginning to appear between 35,000 and 30,000 years ago (Gilligan 2018: 77, 87–88, 102–105).

Cave Art

Finally, we arrive at a time when our ancient ancestors begin almost to speak to us from the caves of Spain and France, and possibly much farther east in Sulawesi. The understanding of the transition from the Neanderthal realm of being to that of anatomically modern humans has grown clearer and fuller in recent decades. The surprising 65,000- and 35,000-year-old geometric designs in Spanish caves made with charcoal and ochre by Neanderthals come close to early signs made by *Homo sapiens* in South Africa around the same time – and not very much later in Europe (Hoffmann et al. 2018). Caves in Sulawesi have recently been discovered with images of warty pigs and hand stencils (45,000 years old), as well as similar cave paintings (35,000 years old) made by anatomically modern humans (Brumm et al. 2021). These are found along what must have been migration routes leading into New Guinea and Australia, so that archaeologists are confident they will find more such evidence soon (Aubert et al. 2014). Early Aurignacian remains found in a Portuguese cave from 41,000 to 38,000 years ago, and cave paintings and carvings in Chauvet-Pont d'Arc Cave, France dating back to around 38,000 years ago, attest to the presence of modern humans. Neanderthals were probably still around in some southern European areas not long before Chauvet, for example, at three cave sites in Southern Iberia (Spain and Portugal) dating from around 37,000 years ago, and still performing culturally and technologically as they had done up until their disappearance.

The degree of overlap and interchange between these two populations is uncertain. Jonathan Haws and colleagues describe the last refuges of Neanderthal populations in the Iberian Peninsula at the time of anatomically modern human advances across Eurasia. Current archaeological data places modern humans in the Balkan Peninsula at Bacho Kiro some 46,000 years ago and posits a rapid spread from there up the Danube and along the Mediterranean rim. This was probably a mosaic process that included encounters with Neanderthals. Around 43,000 to 42,000 years ago these various streams coalesced into a common Aurignacian culture and technology. This was a period of severe cold and dry periods that disrupted habitats and caused a southward expansion of Eurosiberian fauna along the Atlantic coast and the east–west river drainages of the Duero and Tagus. And as we have seen, serious consequences also included depopulation and the ultimate disappearance of Neanderthals (Haws et al. 2020).

From this point on, anatomically modern humans established themselves firmly in Europe, responding to fluctuations between glacial advances and interglacial warming periods by moving with plant and animal communities. Their technological developments and cultural adaptations included increasingly precise stone tools, naturalistic bone carvings, geometrical signs, complex clothing, mats, nets and baskets made from plants, and the spectacular cave art capturing visions of the great animals that surrounded them. The main waves of modern human migrations into Europe are outlined and mapped by David Reich (2018: 87–92), based on ancient DNA studies that have supported, sharpened, and in some ways upended generations of archaeological studies.

- First, as we have seen, came the Aurignacian consolidation of pioneer population waves, which spread from central Europe around 45,000 years ago after their arrival from the Levant northward from the Balkan area. They moved as far east as Russia, west into northern Europe, and down into the Iberian Peninsula, remaining in those areas for 20,000 years.
- The Gravettian migration was a subgroup of the earliest arrivals from north of the Black Sea, who moved west and south from around 33,000–20,000 years ago, coming to dominate Europe by displacing and/or merging with the Aurignacians. Their art included musical instruments such as bone flutes, portable female statuettes of stone and bone, and baked clay figurines of humans and animals such as mammoth, bear, fox, lion, horse, and woolly rhinoceros. Impressions in the clay at some sites show they made textiles and baskets from plant materials such as flax, though that practice was probably long-established by previous people (von Petzinger 2016: 106–109).[12]

---

[12] Following archeological traditions, Genevieve von Petzinger (2016): 135) defines Solutreans as a distinct cultural group that moved south into Iberian and other southern European refuges around 22,000 –17,000 years ago during the Last Glacial Maximum when the glaciers advanced again to cover northern Europe. In Reich's outline, this group is essentially the latter stage of the Gravettian.

- Magdalenian peoples were those who moved back northward into France and Germany 19,000–14,000 years ago from their warm Iberian refuges along with plants and their wider animal community as the ice sheets retreated for the last time. Their cave art was more refined in some respects than the work of earlier periods (Reich 2018: 87–92; von Petzinger 2016: 134–139). The dates of some Magdelenian sites (e.g. Niaux, 17,000–11,000; Robin Hood's Cave, UK horse on bone, 12,500–13,000; Lascaux, 19,000; Trois Frères, 13,000) overlap with the beginnings of Anatolian Neolithic which we will examine more closely in Section 4.
- A final movement, caused by a major climate warming called the Bølling–Allerød which melted the Alpine glacial blockage of the northern Mediterranean coast 14,000 years ago, brought a surge of plants and animals from southeastern Europe and the Near East into southwestern Europe and northward. This surge included human groups that, Reich (2018) says, "had waited out the ice age in southern Europe [and then] became dominant across the entire European continent" (87–93).

Two archaeological sites preserve almost continuous records of these movements: the Goyet Cave in Belgium and the Monte Castillo Cave in Portugal. Cave art suddenly ended during drastic climate change oscillations at the end of the Last Glacial Maximum some 11,000 years ago (Reich 2018: 89–93; von Petzinger 2016: 137–141).

All of these population groups were related hunter and gathering cultures, each new branch moving in gradually and replacing or perhaps partially absorbing the previous genetic heritage. However, I shall argue that genetic markers alone do not tell the whole story, and that cultural exchange and inheritance continued among these people as thousands of years passed by. The behaviors and patterns of Aurignacians must have been shared and mingled with those of the Gravettians and those of the Magdalenian groups as they adapted to the changing landscapes and plant and animal communities around them. The fact that they were all descendants of related European hunter–gatherer groups that began arriving from the Levant some 50,000 or slightly more years ago suggests that they shared cultural habits from those beginnings and could have intermingled with each other much more easily than with Neanderthals.

Yet the sudden appearance of cave art at Chauvet, Les Trois Frères, Niaux, Lascaux, Altamira, and so many other places stuns us with its sudden realism and power after the millennia of archaic ancestors whose views of their world are lost in darkness. After moving along narrow passages winding through calcite formations far from the daylight world, it is a shock to see handprints outlined by red ochre – the apparent signatures of people like us announcing their presence from a lost world. We are awed by panoramas of vanished beasts in motion – aurochs, woolly mammoths, bison, woolly rhinoseros, lions, bears, horses, reindeer, and huge archaic deer. How did they suddenly appear? Why did these ancient people venture so far underground to record visions or sometimes almost photographic images of all these creatures from the vast herds they followed and hunted? Nicaraguan poet Ernesto Cardenal writes of the caves in *Versos del Pluriverso*,

> Nos fascina Altamira
> Sin entenderla
> Y somos los mismos
> Somos los mismos de las cavernas
> Los ahora llamados civilizados.
> Biológicamente somos los mismos
> . . .
> No sabemos nada de lo soñado en esas cuevas
> Pero esas cuevas están en nuestros sueños.
>
> [Altamira fascinates us
> without our understanding it.
> And we are the same.
> We are the same as those of the caves
> Those now called civilized.
> Biologically we are the same.
> . . .
> We know nothing about what was dreamed of in these caves
> But these caves are in our dreams.]
>
> (Cardenal 2013: 64)

We are the same, yet not the same, as Cardenal realizes, and these images still haunt our deep memories and imaginations.

Hominins used caves for thousands of years as shelters, as we have seen from the examples of Goyet in Belgium and Monte Castillo in Portugal, which both contain multiple levels of human activity from 25,000 to over 100,000 years. Geographical range is indicated by caves in Sulawesi in Indonesia, Denisova in the Siberian Altai, Gibraltar, and Spain. South African cave sites have yielded some of the very earliest "drawings" in ochre, as well as even earlier evidence from 100,000 to 70,000 years ago of the grinding of pigments for such markings in the Blombos Cave and in the Diepkloof Rock Shelter where geometrically decorated ostrich shells have been excavated from layers ranging from 85,000 to 52,000 years old (von Petzinger 2016: 58–70). The oldest plant fibers spun or twisted into cord by humans were found in the Kvavadze Cave in the Republic of Georgia, dated at 23,000 years old (St. Clair 2018: 21–24).

In these caves, people butchered animals, carved stone and bone, worked hides and made clothing from them, tended fires, and probably sheltered from the coldest and wettest weather. But they did not live in the caves continually, and they stayed close to the entrances for their habitation. For one thing, they had to share these retreats with other animals such as hibernating cave bears, cave lions, and wolves who might have been preying on each other. Bones and cave bear hibernation nests deep in Chauvet Cave suggest as much. And many of the paintings on the cave walls are scored with clawmarks of bears, who were obviously using the caves after humans had been there to create their art (Chauvet et al. 1996: 44–66). Humans hunted aurochs, mammoths, horses, and reindeer just as these other predators did, in a complex mutualism that included using landscape features for protection. They watched each other and performed parallel activities, careful mutual avoidance, and occasional conflict just as the apex predators of Africa still do around the great herds of the Serengeti or in the Ngorongoro Crater of Tanzania. So the human uses of caves must have included some competition with bears, lions, hyenas, and wolves in which fire may have played a part, because hearths made of big pieces of charcoal have been found on the floors near the paintings. Some researchers suggest that humans learned from wolves in a mutualism that helped shape our social behavior and strategies for hunting in groups (Schleidt and Shalter 2003: 59–60). Their gradual coevolution with us resulted in the appearance of domestic dogs around 25,000 years ago.

But these people were migratory hunters and foragers who followed the herds seasonally and during changing climates. They spent much of their time in more open landscapes, at camps with varying kinds of structures. Not all Paleolithic people had access to caves, for example those on the Central Eurasian Plains at sites such as Dolni Vestonice and Petrkovice in Moravia; and Kosienki and Sungir in Russia. There, archaeologists have found burials from the Aurignacian period, of people decorated with elaborate patterns of perforated shells that must have been attached to leather clothing that has long since disappeared. Also kilns were found and pottery figurines of humans and other animals (Cook 2013: 62–71, 117–130). Remains indicate that strong shelters of made from mammoth bones and skins were built for protection against the cold weather of the winter months (Gilligan 2018: 206–209). In Europe itself, archaeologists Margaret Conkey and Kathleen Stirling's "Between the Caves" project has focused on the site of Peyre Blanque in the Pyrenees, near the important French caves of Niaux, Marsoulas, and Mas d'Azil. This habitation site is where the Magdalenian people who decorated the caves probably gathered and stayed, as a node among pathways of movement around the region. Remains of stone structures, tools, pigments such as iron oxide (ochre), and animal bones reveal hints of the ordinary lives whose activities are not preserved in the caves.[13]

The variety of early human dwelling places, about which we have only fragmentary evidence, nevertheless indicates that they chose sites where they could be safe but also close to the ecological resources necessary for their lives. Monte Castillo in Portugal was typical in being located where animal migrations could be seen from a high vantage point. For thousands of years it gave access to environmental information and affordances that were ideal for human flourishing. In such places, people could act out their central functions within the wider animal and plant community, moving when necessary to follow the seasons and changes in the landscape along with other animals. The hills, rivers, open plains, wooded areas, and cliffs with their caves all made up the sense of a home space, as Maher and Conkey (2019) suggest in their commentary on the Paleolithic hunter–gatherer site of Peyre Blanque in the Pyrenees and the Epipaleolithic site of Kharaneh IV in present-day Israel. These ways of living shaped familiar landscapes as they continue to do for indigenous hunting and foraging groups like the Achuar people of Ecuador among whom anthropologist Philippe Descola lived in the 1970s, and the Hadza people of the Lake Eyasi region of Tanzania today. For the Achuar and their neighbors in the forest regions of the South American lowlands, as Descola (2013) explains, no clear ontological distinctions are made between humans and the other beings around them. "Most of the entities that people the world are interconnected in a vast continuum inspired by unitary principles and governed by an identical regime of sociability" (9).

Descola carefully analyzes belief systems and ecological understandings among many tribal peoples from China to the Americas, demonstrating the distinctive ways in which they think of the continuum of life and how to preserve respectful relationships within it. This account of life accords with Timothy Ingold's (2000) characterization of present-day hunter–gatherers' ways of perceiving the world as a community of persons, in which humans and animals are ontologically equivalent "as organism-persons and as fellow participants in a life process" (51). There is no privileged observer outside of this dynamic field of relations, but instead all beings watch each other in reciprocal activities of learning to see what is revealed (55). Although we cannot extrapolate backward in time some 30,000 thousand years to know what Paleolithic humans thought of their relationships with other animals, something like this kind of understanding must have been the norm for them,

---

[13] See www.peyreblanque.org.

expressed in their depiction of great animals on the cave walls of France and Spain.

Furthermore, cave art could not have suddenly appeared from nowhere. Evidence from Java, Africa, and the Levant indicates that it was part of a long and gradual development. An engraved shell from Java dated between 430,000 and 540,000 years ago made by *Homo erectus,* the grinding of colors from mineral stones in Zambia between 260,000 and 300,000 years ago, and the symbolic figurine of a human female from 230,000 years ago found at Berekhat Ram in Israel are only a few examples that prefigure the cave art 200,000 years later (von Petzinger 2016: 31–36). However, the widespread cave art of Paleolithic Europe does represent the first rich body of representational painting and sculpture that captures a world of animals we can recognize and a way of seeing that feels close to our own.

As Alexander Marshack showed decades ago with groundbreaking microscopic photography, portable art from these caves scratched or engraved on bones and stones captured the knowledge of spawning salmon and other fish, snakes, flowering and seeding plants, and many other environmental elements during significant seasonal periods. Small bone and antler sculptures also represent the same animals in the cave paintings, as well as birds and other animals (Cook 2013: 156–221; Marshack 1972: 207, 211–214, 223–228, 252–271). The earliest volcanic eruption ever pictured may be found on the wall of the Chauvet-Pont d'Arc Cave, which was thirty-five kilometers southeast of strombolian volcanic activity at the time and could have been seen at night from hills near the cave entrance (Nomade et al. 2016; Calloway 2016; Chauvet et al. 1996: 26, 61, 92). Marshack also challenged archaeological tradition with his theories about lunar calendrical records carved into bones, although they remain controversial (see Robinson 1992).[14]

Most commentators have thought the painted caves were religious sanctuaries, but perhaps that is too much of a projection of our own sense of the sacred. It is nevertheless significant that the cave paintings are usually so deep within the caves, far from the daylight world. As Cardenal (2013: 60) says, these paintings and carvings were invisible to anyone venturing inside without the knowledge, care, and controlled fire for illumination. Many are palimpsests, with images superimposed upon each other at different times, so there must have been a performative, ritual quality to the act of painting. Marshack's use of infrared photography brought this quality into clear attention for the first time in the 1970s. Materials such as ochre and charcoal had to be brought deep inside and

---

[14] Markings on cave walls and incised bones from very early periods are often described as the beginnings of writing, but we cannot explore that topic here (see, for example, Davis-Marks 2021; von Petzinger 2016).

ground into powder, mixed with binding material and applied with sticks or brushes or fingers. We shall never know exactly what they or the performance of their creation meant, but they clearly show a fascinated attention to the animal life around them, a world of marvelous fellow creatures whose bodies and movements filled their imaginations. They knew them so well that they could represent them vividly from imaginative inner images. This is mimicry of a profound clarity, familiarity, and respect. The great aurochs, mammoths, bison, horses, reindeer, rhinoceros, lions, and bears are the beings they wanted to take into the secret places of Earth and recreate to witness again and again, perhaps in some sense of dreaming.

Even now, when we modern urban people enter the caves, we are dwarfed by the presence and numbers of these animals, as at Chauvet where a group of huge lions moves toward rhinoceros and bison,[15] or Lascaux, where aurochs and horses move along the high walls of sinuous passages.[16] The few human images of the earliest Aurignacian and Gravettian caves are only tiny figures dancing in hybrid forms or disguises among many larger beasts, as at the French caves of Lascaux, Peche Merle, Les Trois Frères, and the Laugerie Basse rock shelter and the Italian Fumani Cave near Verona. In all these places humans seem to move amid the great animals in some kind of homage or communion as they wear the horns of bison or are hybrids with both bovine and human body parts. Later on, however, during the Magdalenian period, the images show animals attacked, wounded, and bleeding (Marshack 1972: 235–258). A famous example is a scene from Lascaux of the stylized figure of a man with the head of a bird and an erect penis, lying on his back beneath a huge wounded bison or bull.

Female images are ubiquitous from the very early Aurignacian through the Magdalenian cultures. These have traditionally been called "voluptuous" but are probably not to be considered in such terms. These were the bodies that brought forth new life, and they are associated with similar phenomena in the surrounding animal community. Male figures appear as well, as we have seen, and there are bone carvings representing penises associated with serpents and fish. But for the most part, human images are female, often pregnant and sometimes related to similar animal forms; in one carved example, a pregnant female lies on her back beneath a reindeer, and in another two examples, women, one pregnant, crawl along one side of a polished bone, with two bison on the other side (Cook 2013: 228–229). André Leroi-Gouran created an elaborate theory of gendered signs and

---

[15] See https://archeologie.culture.fr/chauvet/en.

[16] See https://archeologie.culture.fr/lascaux/en/visit-cave.

images in which female representations predominated (Leroi-Gouran 1967: 512–514), though more recent archaeological thinking has complicated that view. Marshack's photographs show many kinds of carvings indicating breasts and pubic areas, some fairly realistic and some highly stylized. And of course there are the famous "Venus" figures from Willendorf and Dolni Vestonice (Cook 2013: 31–45, 60–105; Marshack 1972: 281–340). Whatever exact purpose and meanings they carried, these female carvings and images are important preludes to Neolithic cultures in central Europe and Anatolia.

Special attention has always been paid to the several "sorcerer" or "shaman" figures in cave paintings and sculptures ranging from Fumani Cave (34,000–32,000 years old), to Holenstein-Stadel Cave and Hohle Fels Cave in Germany (35,000 years old) and Chauvet-Pont d'Arc Cave (37,000 years old) (Cook 2013: 40–41), Lascaux (19,000 years old), and Trois Frères in France (13,000 years old). Marshack (1972: 272–275) includes a number of similar depictions engraved on bone or antler. Regardless of whether these hybrid figures represent ecstatic shamanic rituals, as many commentators have suggested, they do obviously signify a desired fusion of a human body with that of a powerful animal (see Clottes and Lewis-Williams 1998).

Two of the earliest carved images from the Hohlenstein-Stadel (40,000 years old) and Hohle Fels Caves (35,000 years old) are "lion-men" in ivory, with bodies that gracefully combine both feline and human formal qualities. With the more complete and well-carved body of the Hohle Fels figure, in particular, the arms look human from the front but more feline in profile and from the rear, while the legs have clearly human contours in the thighs, knees, and calves. The head is undeniably that of a lion with pricked ears and long muzzle (Cook 2013: 28–37).

From a similar time period, a figure in Chauvet Cave is a strange fusion of a large dark bison head in profile above the lower half of a female human facing forward with the pubic region almost the size of the bison head and rendered in black charcoal like the head, with legs on either side in the reddish-orange color of the limestone background, their shape outlined in black. The bison's left front leg blends into the female's left leg. This is the only known "painted" woman of the late Aurignacian–early Gravettian transitional period. The better-known figures of hybrid male dancers with bison or stag horns are found on the walls of Trois Frères Cave and Fumani Cave, the latter being only a schematic figure in ochre, with outstretched arms and horns. The famous Lascaux figure, wounded or in an ecstatic trance, has the head of a bird (Cook 2013: 57; Marsack 1972: 272–277).

At a 30,000 to 40,000 year remove from our own world, these figures seem weird and impossible to interpret in any specific way. Jill Cook's remarks about the meaning of the lion-man sculptures summarize some of the possibilities of meaning for all these hybrid creatures.

> As an actor, the Lion Man could have been a totem symbolizing kinship with a spirit being with leonine attributes, which might have been regarded as a creator, ancestor, protector, companion or helper who assisted in the dialogue with the vital forces of life considered to be fixed in the environment. If these forces are thought to be everywhere in the landscape, as in animistic beliefs, such a fantastic being might reflect efforts to connect to the supernatural via a spirit being in human/animal guise. (Cook 2013: 35).

Both this figure and others are found deep in the caves' most secret places, leading to the inference that they carry particularly intense value or force. They project human participation in the much larger worlds of these more powerful animals, the possibility of sharing some of their qualities, or the wish to do so. No sense of rupture is indicated here, rather a deeply intimate connection.

In her book *The Imaginary of Animals* French philosopher Annabelle Dufourcq (2022) describes an inherited "intersubjective quest" between humans and other animals that haunts our imaginations. Other animals "launch a process of active de-centering and a quest for meaning that we inherit. Human beings seek themselves in non-human animals . . . and they in others, including us" (166). Such a claim contests the continued insistence of thinkers such as Heidegger, Rilke, Lacan, and Agamben on the abyssal difference between humans and other animals, in which humans are not even animals. Dufourcq calls this a fantasy about the alleged extraordinary nature of our species and a failure to pay attention to all the ways we have always existed in intertwined relationships with other animals. She asserts that animality is fundamentally characterized by an existential, fractured identity and an openness to the virtual which results from it. The images and symbols of nonhuman animals "invade our dreams, our works of art, and our everyday metaphors: They meddle in our language and thoughts" (Dufourcq 2022: 168–169). The humans who painted the caves during the Paleolithic era that led to our own were expressing an understanding of their long involvement with members of the wider animal community. From a Gestalt perspective, influenced by Merleau-Ponty's thinking, Dufourcq (2022) explains that, "At stake is the possibility of conceiving of a shared thinking life between humans and animals. Beneath the surface of apparently clearly differentiated realms, Gestalten constitute a unique and common ontological root" (99). Our Paleolithic ancestors must have felt this at a profound level, which shaped their need to paint that shared life, with images of mimicry in hybrid combinations of human and horned animal forms dancing among the great beasts, on surfaces deep in the Earth.

The cave culture that projected and enacted such visions of shared interanimality for 30,000 years came to a close with the Bølling–Allerød climate change beginning around 14,000 years ago. New migrations from the southeast spread a very different ancestry across Europe in the next few thousand years. According to David Reich (2018), these people, who had waited out the ice age in southern Europe, "became dominant across the entire European continent following the melting of the Alpine glacial wall" (92–93). What happened to the Magdalenian hunters and foragers who painted the last panoramas in the caves? Probably they followed the herds of reindeer, woolly mammoths, and aurochs to the north as suddenly warmer weather changed the tundra into forests. Or perhaps the climate warming was too sudden for them to adapt, and they died out as the Neanderthals had done because of climactic changes (Ghose 2016; Strickland 2018). The new groups from southern Europe seemingly had no interest in caves but established their own nomadic hunting, gathering, and fishing practices as they moved into the warmer climates of the newly forested landscapes and up to the game-rich marshy lowlands of northern Europe which, at that time, formed an uninterrupted continent all the way to the west of what are now the British Isles and northeast over the Scandinavian and Baltic regions. Between what are now Scotland and Norway stretched a wide expanse of hills, marshlands, and heavily wooded valleys called Doggerland. There was no break between France and Ireland, though the sea gradually rose as glacial melting continued and eventually formed the English Channel and Irish Sea. During the same period of several thousand years ago, the sea began to submerge Doggerland, creating the North Sea that now separates Britain, the Netherlands, Denmark, and Scandanavia.

In the Levant, around 13,000 years ago, Natufian hunter–gatherers began gradually settling into villages that were at first base camps along migratory pathways – nodes of the kind Conkey, Maher, and Sterling document with respect to hunter and gathering peoples in Paleolithic times. Burial practices sometimes included skull removal and decoration, presaging similar activities later at Çatalhöyük. Natufians harvested a wide range of wild grasses, pulses, and fruits according to seasonal availability and hunted gazelle, deer, cattle, and wild boar in coastal areas, while horses and ibex were hunted in the steppe areas to the east. Water fowl and fish were part of the diet along the Jordan valley and around Hula Lake. Gradually, probably in response to the worsening climate of the Younger Dryas cold period from 11,000 to 10,300 years ago, they began deliberate cultivation of wild grains in a more sedentary pattern of life where wild resources were concentrated. Long patterns of cultural and material exchange between the Levant and northern areas of Jordan, Syria, and southern Anatolia meant that these movements toward a more sedentary life were shared in many areas. Anatolian obsidian found at Jericho and other Natufian sites indicate patterns of exchange which also later appear in the development of pottery (Bar-Yosef 1990: 162–170; Mellaart 1966: 9–15).

Health Consequences of Sedentism

Hunter–gatherer peoples lived mobile lives following the changing climates and seasonal patterns of the animal and plant communities around them. Their populations were relatively sparse and small, with their main health problems coming from parasitic worms, zoonotic or cross-species diseases that would have been sporadic, and vector-borne diseases like malaria that have left copious evidence in our genes such as the propensity for sickle-cell anemia (Harper 2021: 91–104). But because of low population density and mobility, these diseases did not have the opportunity to spread widely. The development of sedentary communities and agriculture changed all that. Kyle Harper's (2021) deep historical study, *Plagues upon the Earth: Disease and the Course of Human History*, charts this progress of disease from the Pleistocene to the present era.

Infectious diseases associated with human waste and close living conditions, as well as domestic animals gathered in groups nearby or even within living areas, found ideal conditions for spreading and many insect communities to take advantage of concentrated animal waste. These living situations also drew other creatures into commensal relationships with human hosts. "Commensal animals like rats and mice, pigeons and sparrows, are perfectly suited to live in the nooks and crannies of human-altered habitats," writes Harper (2021: 134). They have coevolved with us since the late Neolithic period, even before large cities, when there were already outbreaks of cholera and typhoid, and zoonotic diseases such as smallpox moved back and forth between humans and cattle. Farming involved the transformation of environments and a host of negative feedbacks (Harper 2021: 122–157; Gilligan 2018: 130–144). As Harper (2021) explains, "In the early Neolithic, the paradox of progress played out in the bowels of the first farmers. In the next wave of technical advance, brought on by metals and more complex forms of social organization, the scene of action moved from our guts to our lungs" (157).

Epidemics became frequent in large cities, with Rome standing as Harper's major example. The empire's success in conquest and technology brought benefits still celebrated in Western history, but it did not bring health. "Roman society was simply helpless in the face of infectious disease. The poor health of the Romans is written all over their bones. The rise of Roman civilization made people shorter by an average of several centimeters" because they were "prosperous but sick" (Harper 2021: 192). Famous examples of epidemics can be found in the likely typhoid outbreak in Athens from 430–433 BCE (Littman 2009) and a smallpox epidemic during the reign of Marcus Aurelius around 165 CE, but we have particularly detailed historical accounts of the bubonic plague that struck Constantinople and then Italy beginning in 541 CE in the reign of Justinian (Harper 2021: 193–195). We now know from ancient DNA studies of the bones of Yamnaya migrants 5,000 years ago that *Yersinia pestis* was brought into Europe from Central Asia much earlier (Reich 2018: 113–114). Still, the variety of the plague that struck Justinian Rome was of a fresh potency, causing huge mortality that spread throughout the Roman Empire (Harper 2021: 209–219). Historical records from that time onward offer a continuous story of our species' struggles with the maladies we have always shared with the ecosystems in which we live, but which gradually became much more varied and virulent beginning with the period to which we now turn, when humans began to separate themselves into enclosures and tried to control the natural world. The long history of human diseases is a profound testimony to our embeddedness and interactions within animal, insect, fungal, bacterial, and viral ecosystems. It is an intimate, continuously evolving interanimality that moves across species boundaries with unceasing adaptability.

4 Monumental Architecture, Towns, and Cultural Separation from Wildness

Our attention now turns to Anatolia, where the first known permanent large structures and sculptures and the first towns created the circumstances where animals and plants began to be systematically controlled. Hunter–gatherers who still moved around early Holocene landscapes in seasonal patterns began to create stone monuments at Göbekli Tepe and Nevali Cori in what is now southern Turkey, near the headwaters of the Euphrates. In the late 1990s German archaeologist Klaus Schmidt upended standard theories about the development of agriculture with his discoveries of these huge buildings that seemed like open-air temples created by hunter–gatherers before permanent settlements or agriculture. Farther to the west, and one thousand or two thousand years later, Çatalhöyük and Hacilar became sedentary villages that developed into settled towns lasting more than 1,000 years. Here, in the early 1960s, archaeologist James Mellaart uncovered some six layers of habitation with closely connected domestic buildings that had strange sculptures, animal skulls, and remarkable large wall frescoes. Troubles with the Turkish government prevented further explorations for almost thirty years until British archaeologist Ian Hodder began new work that continues at present.

The final section of our deep historical exploration will focus on these remarkable Anatolian sites and then close by considering their cultural descendants some 6,000 to 4,000 years later in Mesopotamia and Greece, where human voices finally reach us directly in the first known literary epic and a tragedy based on one of the earliest Greek deities. *The Epic of Gilgamesh* and Euripides' *Bacchae* both continue a fascination with human–animal relations focused on the bull as representative of wild natural forces, which is central to the art of Göbekli Tepe and Çatalhöyük, and recall the enormous wild power of great animals in the Paleolithic cave paintings of southern Europe. Both express deeply conflicted attitudes about the human place in environments that had, until relatively recently, been home territories shared with all the animal communities but now seem separate, dangerous, and needing to be controlled by heroic human will.

James Mellaart's excavations at Hacilar and Çatalhöyük revealed many stone and clay female images that led him to characterize these Neolithic towns as centers of a "mother goddess" culture. Some of the figurines, especially those found at Hacilar, are reminiscent of the Paleolithic sculptures from European caves discussed earlier. Many are full-bodied, in a hieratic pose with hands under breasts, like those found in succeeding sites all over the Middle East (Museum Staff n.d.: 30, 32–33, 51, 74–76; Gimbutas 1982). Stone grinding tools and grain storage containers at these sites supported Mellaart's theories that the female figures were associated with fertility of both wild and domesticated plants and animals. Traditional thinking held that the production of food surpluses stimulated the building of permanent dwellings where grains could be stored and domesticated animals kept in pens. Recent discoveries of stone grinding tools in Italy, Russia, and Czechoslovakia going back 30,000 years have complicated that picture, revealing that Gravettian humans made flour from cattail roots, ferns, and wild grains. The grindstones bear the starchy remains of plants, and some were also used for grinding ochre (Revedlin et al. 2010). These were clearly practices among mobile hunting and gathering people that long predated plant domestication and settled agriculture.

German archaeologist Klaus Schmidt upset the received story with his discovery of the strange monoliths and associated stone buildings at Göbekli Tepe dating back 11,500 years. These seem to have been open-air, circular structures of huge limestone stelae on terrazzo floors surrounded by stone walls. Schmidt found no signs of domestic dwellings but rather the remains of communal feasting sites full of the bones of wild animals such as gazelles, boars, red deer, and water birds. The stone pillars are flat and T-shaped. Some are anthropomorphic, carved with flat stylized arms and hands on abdomens and stylized belts or skirts but without heads. Instead, most bore carved reliefs of fierce male animals such as bulls, boars, lions, bears, wolves or foxes, and whole nests of venomous snakes. Stylized figures of some water birds such as cranes and ducks also appear. These stelae reach three or more meters tall and weigh up to ten tons. They were picked out of the surrounding bedrock with stone tools, then moved on rollers and ramps to be raised into place. Schmidt called one of the buildings (Enlosure B) "a Mesopotamian Stonehenge in the making" (Schmidt 2007: 70, 134–136), though it predated the British Stonehenge by almost 8,000 years. Ritualized infilling of these sites before abandonment preserved the interiors with their stelae and carvings.

The imagery of this place is insistently masculine and aggressive, with at least several human figures displaying erect penises. Some of the human carvings are lacking a head, and incised human skulls have recently been discovered at the site (Gresky et al. 2017; Schmidt 2007: 150, 246). Schmidt considered it a sanctuary meant to be seen far above the surrounding plain, with the fierce animal sculptures serving a protective function as allies of the humans who built the cultic centers. One exception is a kind of stone totem pole with what appears to be the figure of a birthing woman and a baby beneath her. Another is an incised figure of a female with splayed legs displaying, as Schmidt describes, enlarged sexual organs, or perhaps being penetrated by what seems a schematic penis (Schmidt 2007: 223; Hodder 2006: 200, 202). It is very difficult to know exactly what these figures mean, and how potent human males are related to the animals and the minimal female presence at the site. We can be certain, however, that humans are dominant figures for whom the dangerous wild male animals are totemic or symbolic associates whose powers are symbolically absorbed by the huge anthropomorphic pillars. They assert monumental powers that can be seen from all points of the landscape below. Schmidt thinks this was the setting for a death cult, a place of rituals periodically performed by large gatherings of hunter–gatherers who came together for ceremonial feasting and what Hodder (2006: 29–30, 203) suggests might be a kind of transcendence associated with male violence, sex, and death.

A very different world had previously been uncovered by Mellaart a good distance northwest of Göbekli Tepe at Hacilar (1,000 kilometers away) and at Çatalhöyük (700 kilometers away). Beginning in 1957, Mellaart led the excavation of Hacilar, a Neolithic settlement that lasted from around 8,400–7,700 years ago, where he found evidence of the domestication of both plants and animals and the impressive sculptures of corpulent females mentioned above, some of them holding infants or even, in one case, an animal (Mellaart 1970: 210–213). The discovery of Çatalhöyük was much more significant, because

Mellaart quickly found the remains of a large town made up of closely connected mud-brick houses similar in structure to the Pueblo dwellings of the American Southwest. Here, as many as eighteen levels of inhabitation reached back at least 9,000 years to a time when hunting and gathering peoples settled into substantial permanent buildings, although they continued to practice their traditional ways of finding food. This seemed to Mellaart to be the first real city in history, though many even older towns have since been found in central and eastern Anatolia (Hodder 2007: 106).

What continues to make Çatalhöyük distinctive is that settlement there lasted around 1,400 years with ruins revealing the transition from hunting and gathering patterns to settled agriculture. It is also unique in containing a wealth of art and symbolism concentrated in the house. For the first time since Paleolithic caves, colorful wall paintings of humans and animals appear, though they are much more stylized and less dynamic than the art of the great cave displays. In one wall painting that may be a map of the town, a volcano is shown erupting in the distance, probably Hasan Dag which has recently been dated as having erupted around 9,000 years ago and which would have been visible from the town eighty miles away (Hodder 2006: 163–164; Oskin 2013). As we have seen, similar volcano paintings occur in Chauvet Cave.

The main living areas of houses were decorated with the skulls of bulls (buchrania) protruding from the walls above one another or grouped around a symbolic space. The bones of some animals were plastered into the walls and human burials were placed under sleeping areas. Some human skulls decorated with layers of plaster and paint to look like living heads were found in living areas and some in graves, reminiscent of practices discovered in Natufian settlements and widespread in other areas of Anatolia and the Middle East (Hodder 2006: 146). Painted pottery and sculptures of stone and clay were found in later levels, as well as evidence of symbolically ordered domestic life that included hearths, woven mats for the floors, and storage bins for grains and pulses in side rooms.

Hodder explains that residents of the town built new houses above the remains of earlier ones, having careful dismantled and cleaned them, with the remaining spaces carefully infilled with pebbles or special soils or objects from middens. New walls were built directly above the earlier foundations. These practices were ritualized and symbolic social methods of creating continuity (Hodder 2006: 132). During the inhabitation of each level, walls and floors were continually replastered with white lime. Entrances were openings in the roof over the hearth, with ladders reaching down into the interior where the symbolic arrangement of spaces ordered daily life. The hearth was placed in the south part of the main room, which was "dirty" in comparison to the "clean" north area of raised platforms which were sitting and sleeping places with the burials of ancestors placed beneath them. Family history was thus embodied in material memory shaped by the house itself (Hodder 2006: 17, 117–140).

The distribution and treatment of art followed these spatial arrangements, with painting and sculpture on north, east, and west walls above "clean" areas. Buchrania were plastered and painted over again and again, like the human heads found in the houses or in burials. One carefully plastered and realistically painted human head was found "in the arms of a woman who had been placed in a pit as part of the foundation of a new building" (Hodder 2006: 138; see also 23 and 108). This seems to be a method of materially sedimenting the memory of significant individual animals and humans, as the houses also literally sediment the past of the town.

The impressive large wall paintings represent a very different attitude toward wild animals than the Paleolithic cave art. They are in human structures, controlled and separated from the wider environment of the wild community. As at Göbekli Tepe, for most of Çatalhöyük's history the animals depicted in the art are not those customarily eaten by the town's inhabitants, but rather large wild aurochs and deer or boars. Most animals in the diet were sheep and goats, with much evidence of wild plants and fruits. It is only the final, upper levels of life in the town that offer evidence of domesticated cattle being a regular part of the diet (Hodder 2006: 86–88, 235, 255). Thus, the large paintings of cattle and deer represent powerful wild creatures with symbolic power. They are surrounded by tiny human figures apparently dancing or playing in what Hodder (2006: 31) thinks might have been initiation rites. Almost all of the humans are males, wearing leopard skins around waists or hips. A few carry bows, but no arrows are evident, nor any representation of attack or hunting. Instead the tail of a bull is being pulled in one painting, and the tail, snout, and tongue of a large stag in another (Hodder (2006: 31, 65, 94). The buchrania and deer horns on the walls of many houses must be the skulls of animals that were eventually killed, but they are not as huge and dominant as those in the paintings. However respectfully their heads may have been treated, inside the houses they are captive, their power brought into the human realm.[17]

In the two most widely published wall paintings, a stylized corpulent female figure in a hieratic pose, similar to those of figurines found at upper levels of the excavations, stands at the edge of the action, seeming to preside over the teasing or baiting of the wild bull or stag (Hodder 2006: 31, 94, 156). This detail seems significant in the context of the many female figurines found at Hacilar, and

---

[17] Hodder's (2006: 213, 254) description of erect penises of wild animals in the paintings does not seem supported by published images and photographs. Steven Mithen's (2003: 91–96) interpretation of these settings is much grimmer, describing people trapped in a hellish bestiary.

especially the well-known figure of a large woman found in a grain bin at Çatalhöyük, seated on what looks like a throne between two leopards or lions on whom her hands rest comfortably. Some have suggested that this clay figure shows her giving birth, but the damaged figurine makes that possibility unclear (see photograph in Hodder 2006: 160). An interesting parallel can be found in the rock art of the Altai Mountains of Mongolia, documented by Esther Jacobson-Tepfer in *The Hunter, the Stag, and the Mother of Animals*. In many pecked or engraved scenes of hunting from the late Pleistocene into the Bronze Age, a female figure stands at the edge of the action. Jacobson-Tepfer interprets the early images as the Mother of Animals, and many later ones as birthing figures (Jacobson-Tepfer 2015: 116–145; see also her Element in this series, 2020: 36). Heraldic women figures of this kind are found in primitive art in many parts of the world (Gimbutas 1982; Fraser 1966) and seem to represent women's reproductive power associated with the wider creative powers of the animal and plant world. The guidebook for *The Museum of Anatolian Civilizations* (Museum Staff n.d.) in Ankara includes many photographs of figurines in heraldic poses, as well as those of bulls from Neolithic Anatolia to the later Hittite era, covering some five thousand years.

Hodder disagrees with Mellaart's characterization of these sculptures as Mother Goddesses, seeing the sexual emphases of the art at Çatalhöyük more in terms of Schmidt's description of assertive masculinity at Göbekli Tepe. Many of the clay female figurines at Çatalhöyük were found in middens and disfigured in various ways, but they could have been used for votive or protective purposes and then broken and discarded after their ritual functions (Hodder 2006: 191–195; see also Cauvin 2000: 29–33). The large figurine Mellaart found in a grain bin was clearly an image of power, and many smaller figurines were found near hearths, sometimes sealed in plaster. One had a seed embedded in the center of her back. Such female representations are chiefly found in the upper, later levels of the city "alongside the hunting/baiting symbolism, as domestic production becomes more socially central" (Hodder 2006: 254–255).

Some tentative interpretations are possible. Two limestone figurines show a human seated on a leopard, one is clearly gendered as female by having breasts and what appears to be a skirt of leopard skin, while the other wears a leopard skin as a shawl. In Level II of the excavation, a figurine was found of a woman wearing what seems to be a leopard skin top (Hodder 2006: 157, 185, 207). These contrast with the wall paintings of men wearing belts or flying loin cloths and dancing around bulls and stags. The human figures on the leopards can be related to female "goddess" figures from the later site at Hacilar that Mellaart (1975) describes as seated on leopards and holding leopard cubs (114–115). Hodder (2006) points out that the maternal bond is unusually strong among leopards, with mother and offspring continuing to have reunions after maturation, thus implying an association with human females. He suggests that at Çatalhöyük figures of humans with leopards or other felines seem to be associated with large relief sculptures on walls of facing pairs of leopards and may embody a balance in gendered tensions and between "[the] individual and the collectivity and between the prowess–animal–spirit–hunting and feasting nexus linked to ancestry and domestic production" (153, 207–208). These animals are central presences, respected solitary predators symbolically brought into the house as an ally to share its power and perhaps protect the people inside. The leopard skins worn by men in the wall paintings suggest that they have adopted some of this power.

Large splayed wall reliefs facing frontally were interpreted by Mellaart as birthing women or goddesses, but Hodder thinks they may be human/bear or other animal/human hybrids (Hodder 2006:142, 157, 201; Todd 1976: 52, 54–55; Mellaart 1966: 122–125). The fact that the heads and extremities were removed from these figures makes clear identification difficult, but the prominently marked abdomen and naval, as well as suggestion of a vulva, make the human link more plausible. A likely birthing figure on the "totem pole" at Göbekli Tepe indicates a possible common emphasis, and at Çatalhöyük a skeleton was found in a similar position, recalling those of the Mongolian Altai birthing figures and the heraldic females surveyed in the art of many cultures by Douglas Fraser. This skeleton lacks a head, as is apparently the case with other especially valued individuals, and this one was unusually covered with a plank and phytoliths indicating that a mat or cloth had covered the body. The unusual position is in sharp contrast with the usual position of undisturbed skeletons on their sides with their knees close to the chest (Hodder 2006: 146–147, 154–155, 222–223).

Because there is little sexual dimorphism among these remains, and analysis of bones suggests that men and women seem to have done the same kinds of physical work and eaten the same foods, Hodder (2006) believes there was a balance in social roles (210–211). The art may reflect this balance, with men dancing around powerful wild male animals whose energies are deeply respected but gradually controlled, and women presiding as observers of male initiation rituals but more centrally associated with domestic spaces where food and human life are maintained. The comfortable bodily relations of female figures with leopards suggest a natural affinity, which is in strong contrast to the leaping and dancing figures of tiny men around great bulls and stags whose protruding horns from house walls and remains in middens tell us that they have ultimately been killed and eaten (see Westling 2021:142–143).

Human Voices

Çatalhöyük was abandoned around 7,000 years ago (5,500 BC), and Hodder has described evidence in the landscape around the city indicating deforestation, extensive burning, erosion, and large-scale grazing that changed the environment for the worse (quoted in Hattam 2016). Nevertheless, Hodder (2006) maintains that the symbolism embodied in its art lived on and was "involved in various versions of generalized myths that circulated very widely in Anatolia and the Middle East prior to Çatalhöyük and later into historic times" (164). In the marshy regions between the Tigris and Euphrates Rivers, not long after the end of Çatalhöyük, hunter–gatherers developed agriculture and began to create settlements that emerged as Sumerian culture by around the 4th millennium BC. By 3,000 BC they had developed a written language that allowed the first known literary narratives to be written. Here, at last, we hear the actual voices of people who had inherited the myths and symbolism Hodder characterized as circulating around that ancient region. The bull, powerful females, heroic males, preoccupations with death, and the relationship of humans to wildness and independent natural forces and communities are all centrally present in the first known epic – the tragic story of Gilgamesh, King of Uruk. The story is usually described as a heroic journey of conquest, a young king's path to wisdom, the triumph of civilization against wildness. But increasingly, it looks like a catastrophic ecological reckoning for arrogant human will against the natural environment.

The earliest Sumerian versions of the story concern a likely historical king around 2,750 BC or 100 years earlier, for he appears in the Sumerian king list as the fifth ruler of the First Dynasty of Uruk (George 2003: xxxi). But different versions of his story exist on cuneiform tablets from Sumerian to later Akkadian and Babylonian, and even Hittite scribal centers and libraries covering more than a thousand years of transmission. No version is complete, because each had to be reconstructed from fragments excavated over 150 years and painstakingly translated by several generations of modern scholars. But provisional as the standard Babylonian version may be, it is written language from our earliest urban ancestors. Gilgamesh is their avatar with a sense of place that glories in a walled city and world of agriculture beside the waters of the Euphrates, which is separate from wild areas outside and especially from dangerous mountain landscapes to the east and west. Central to the city's power is Eanna, the temple of the goddess Inanna/Ishtar, a sacred storehouse.

In spite of the young king's pride in the walls of his city, anxieties about wildness are present from the beginning of the epic. Gilgamesh himself behaves like a wild bull, with such epithets in Andrew George's (2003) translation as "wild bull on the rampage," "wild bull of Lugalbanda, suckling of the august Wild Cow, the goddess Ninsun," "a wild bull lording it" (2–3). Gilgamesh is one-third human and two-thirds divine, but the qualities that must have been represented by the buchrania mounted on domestic walls at Çatalhöyük are internalized within the brash young human ruler and allow him to wreak havoc upon his city. The king, who should be a shepherd to his people, heroic in stature and valiant in war, harries the young men of Uruk with contests, letting "no son go free to his father" and no daughter go free to her mother or to her bridegroom. The women complain to the gods about the increasingly unbearable tyranny of the "savage wild bull you have bred in Uruk-the-Sheepfold" (George 2003: 3–4). To counter this behavior, the gods command the creator goddess Aruru to fashion "a *match* for the *storm* of his heart" (George 2003: 5; italics in the original), and she throws a pinch of clay to the ground. Thus Enkidu is born, a wild man covered with matted hair and "with long tresses like those of a woman" that grows as thickly as barley (George 2003: 3–5). He lives in harmony with the wild animals, feeding as they do and protecting them. Wildness is here a peaceful realm disturbed only by human intruders like the trapper whose pits and snares Endiku destroys. Thus, humans are coded as unnatural outsiders in a complete reversal of the urban dynamics of Uruk where wildness is unbearable disorder in the behavior of the "wild bull" Gilgamesh.

Enkidu's destiny comes to him as the "harlot" Shamhat, probably a temple priestess of Inanna/Ishtar (Dalley 1991: 328), who has been sent to civilize him and lead him to the young king. She bares her body before him when he comes with his herd of gazelles to the waterhole, and he lies with her for six days, sating his desire but simultaneously losing his wild strength. The animals suddenly flee from him; he has "defiled his body so pure." He can no longer run with the herd, but he now has reason and wide understanding (George 2003: 7–8). In this strange reversal, human sexuality represents a violation of natural wildness, because Enkidu's coupling with Shamhat breaks his bond with the natural world. In the shepherds' camp his hair is cut, and he learns human behavior, now dressed as a warrior and protecting the humans and their flocks from lions and wolves during the night.

Inanna/Ishtar is a goddess associated with fertility and the sacred power of sex, linking the human realm with the plant world. The *heiros gamos* or sacred marriage ceremony celebrated for thousands of years in Sumer and Babylon was performed by the king and a high priestess representing the goddess in order to ensure fertility in the fields and among the domestic animals. Ordinary human procreation was understood in similar sacred terms. The sacred celebration is underway in Uruk when Enkidu arrives, a festival described both in terms of an ordinary wedding in which the king goes in first to the bride but also as a divine union in which the bed is readied for "the goddess of weddings," and "Gilgamesh, like a god, was set up as substitute" (George 2003: 16).

Why then is Enkidu so outraged upon arriving in Uruk to learn that the king is about to perform this ritual in The House of Marriage? Enkidu is recognized by the townspeople as a rival for Gilgamesh, looking like him but a bit shorter and stronger of bone. Enkidu blocks Gilgamesh from entering the marriage house and they grapple so violently that the walls shudder and the doorjambs shake (George 2003: 16). Suddenly Gilgamesh ends the fight, and the two pledge themselves devoted companions. This masculine bond replaces allegiance to the goddess of fertility and war, and Gilgamesh vows to undertake a heroic journey to the wild cedar forest, home of the gods and protected by the monster Humbaba. The king's desire for conquest and glory erases any reverence for the sacred forest. Enkidu warns Gilgamesh not to venture into this wilderness, where he had known Humbaba in his own wild early days of wandering with his herds. Instead of challenging the terrible monster, he urges Gilgamesh "to keep safe the cedars" (George 2003: 18–19). Heedless of such advice, Gilgamesh arrogantly ventures beyond the domesticated human world to attack the sacred wild realm and its guardian. On their journey he is beset by terrible dreams that he fears have been sent by a god – a mountain crashing down on him, lightning and fires, a ravaging Thunderbird, a terrible bull. These could be seen as a projection of deep cultural fears, but now Enkidu takes a role that reverses his earlier warnings and his original unity with wildness, insisting that they are good omens (George 2003: 30–37). For the audience, this can be nothing but the portent of disaster.

Arriving at the mountain wilderness, the heroes at first stand "marveling at the forest,/gazing at the lofty cedars," delighted by its abundance and the sweetness of its shade. But Enkidu urges Gilgamesh to find and destroy Humbaba quickly, before the chief god Enlil can notice and prevent their attack. When they confront and kill Humbaba the hills tremble, the mountains shake, and ravines run with blood. Gilgamesh tramples the secret abode of the gods, as he and Enkidu cut down the forest and send its timbers down the river for huge building projects in Uruk.

This outrage brings the wrath of the gods, which Enkidu had feared. Gilgamesh turns against Inanna/Ishtar, who sends the Bull of Heaven to exact revenge. The heroes kill the divine beast who embodies the wild strengths previously associated with the king, and Enkidu flings its thigh at the goddess herself (George 2003: 45–52). To balance this sacrilege against the sacred wilderness and its guardian as well as the divine bull, Enkidu, like his monstrous double and the forest he destroyed, must die. Gilgamesh is consumed with grief after the death of his friend. He calls on the people of Uruk and all the animals to mourn with him, tears off his clothes, covers himself in ashes, and reduces himself to a miserable animal wandering in the wilderness (George 2003: 62–71). His journey to the land of the dead to find Enkidu and eternal life is a failure, and he returns a chastened mortal to the city. The epic ends as it began, with the same paean to the king's marvelous city with its brick walls, orchards and fields, and central temple to Innana/Ishtar. Gilgamesh may be remembered as a hero, but the story of his conquests reveals the disastrous consequences of human arrogance against the wild energies of the natural world.

Similar themes concerning the relation of humans to the wild realms and forces outside city walls are central to Euripides' *Bacchae*, embodied in the ancient god Dionysus. He was a Mycenaean Greek deity whose name appears in the Linear-B tablets from Pylos and whose worship was foundational in the development of Greek theater (*The Oxford Classical Dictionary*: 352–353). The story told in Euripides' tragedy was a traditional one, sedimented in many previous versions. The language he uses is the most archaic of any of his plays (Dodds 1960: xxviii–xxix, xxxvi), so that the text is a kind of palimpsest with the historical playwright's version shaped from that earlier material. Its title announces that the god's ecstatic followers are the protagonists in many ways, instructing the audience from the beginning about the meaning of the action as it proceeds.

We should step back for a moment to acknowledge the cultural layering that may underlie some of the conflicting forces in the play. Ancient DNA studies and recent archaeological work have shown that around 9,000 years ago Anatolian farmers began migrating west along the Mediterranean coast, north-east along the Danube River, and east into the Indus Valley. Their culture and agricultural methods gradually transformed all of these areas, reaching Scandinavia and the British Isles around 4,000 BC (Reich 2018: 94–97; Gron et al. 2015; Cunliffe 2012: 144–149; Cunliffe 2008: 88–112). Familiar motifs from Anatolia such as bulls and snakes are prominent in Minoan and early Greek art and religious practice. Long ago, Martin Nilsson demonstrated the deep cultural links between archaic Greece and Mycenaean Crete (Nilsson 1932; see also Matz 1962). The disturbingly powerful snaky presences in Hesiod's *Theogony* and the figure of the goddess Athena are key indicators of this heritage. Even the famous statue of the goddess by Phidias shows her decorated by snakes and having a huge serpent rising behind her shield as a warning of her power to worshippers and beholders. In Euripides' play, Dionysus and his cousin King Pentheus have snakes, bulls, and lions in their genealogies. Dionysus is called the "bull-headed god " (ταυρόκερων θεὸν) by the Maenads, "crowned with huge serpents"(στεφάνωσέν τε δρακόντων) at his birth (Dodds 1960: 7). He becomes a raging bull when Pentheus attempts to have him captured. Pentheus' father is named Echion, meaning "the Snake," recalling his birth from the dragon's teeth sown by Kadmus (Bagg 1978: 8). Both Kadmus and his daughter Agave are turned into snakes by Dionysus at the end of the play. Human/animal hybrids and metamorphoses haunt the action and resurface in disturbing visions to destabilize species boundaries and practical certainties about human identity. Translator Robert Bagg (1978) speaks of "Euripides's bitter vision of an implacable presence not outside, but *within* our nature, a presence utterly hostile to what we uneasily call our humanity" (14).

A striking difference between this play and the story of Gilgamesh is the divine, inhuman status of Dionysus. Unlike a hero who begins as part god but ends as a chastened mortal, Dionysus only takes human form in order to punish the family of his cousin Pentheus for refusing to acknowledge his divinity. He retains all of his supernatural powers throughout the drama, controlling his female followers, changing his shape from man to uncontrollable bull, and causing fire and earthquake to strike the Theban palace, as well as hallucinatory experiences in Pentheus' mind (Bagg 1978: 9, 40–41; Dodds 1960: 25–26, 148–151). Most crucially for our purposes, the nature of Dionysus' divine association is the opposite of Gilgamesh's vaunting of human conquest over wildness. As Dodds (1960) explains, he is "much more significant and much more dangerous than a wine-god"; he is the principle of animal life, *tauros* (ταυρος, bull) and *taurophagos* (ταυροφαγος, bull-eater), "hunted and the hunter – the unrestrained potency which man envies in the beasts and seeks to assimilate" (xx). More than that, he is *Dendrites* (Δενδριτης, the Power in the tree), *Karpios* (Καρπιος, the fruit-bringer), *Phleus* (Φλευς the abundance of life), "all the mysterious and uncontrollable tides that ebb and flow in the life of nature" (xii).

Young King Pentheus, hypermasculine doppelgänger for his beautiful and epicene cousin Dionysus, is determined to stamp out the offensive worship of the god who has caused the women of Thebes to abandon their homes, their babies, and their domestic duties to go out into the countryside and frolic. Pentheus imagines sexual orgies, in a fevered projection of what seem to be his own repressed urges. The Chorus tells us how to appraise this arrogant young man:

> There is evil in Pentheus' blood–
> the bestial earth blazes in his face,
> an inhuman snake-face
> like those his giant fathers had,
> those butchers who were beaten
> when they tried to fight gods. (Bagg 1978: 37)

A herdsman who has witnessed the townswomen's Bacchic revels contradicts Pentheus' prurient fantasies by describing miraculous harmonies with the Earth's bounties. The women are peaceful, chastely dressed, nursing the young of gazelles and wolf cubs as snakes lick their faces. They decorate each other's hair with ivy and oak leaves and flowers. Water flows from rocks where they strike their wands, or wine from the pasture. Milk flows from the Earth where their fingers scrape, and honey drips from their wands. But male intruders disturb these activities and the women suddenly leap into rage and violence, led by Pentheus' mother, Agave. The dark side of the god is revealed as rampaging Maenads chase men and tear cows to pieces, eating their raw flesh in the ancient Dionysian rituals of *sparagmos* and *omophagia* (Bagg 1978: 43–44).

Pentheus refuses to heed this report and turns on the Stranger. Dionysus teases and enrages him, so that Pentheus tries to tie him up and have him thrown into prison. This is the point at which the Stranger turns into a wild bull and brings earthquake and fire to punish the sacrilege. In Pentheus' confusion over these strange events, the Stranger suddenly offers him the chance to spy on the Maenads at their worship, puncturing Pentheus' self-control so completely that he agrees to dress as a woman and be led to the wild meadows where the god's revels continue. In his now blurred vision, Pentheus sees the Stranger trotting like a bull, with horns sprouting from his head. Illusions of clear human/animal distinctions are erased here, as is Pentheus' sense of his own boundaries.

The fatal climax happens offstage when the Maenads catch sight of Pentheus spying from atop a pine tree and tear it down, ripping him to pieces as he begs for his life and screams in his death. Led by his mother, they devour his raw flesh in ecstasy and Agave proudly claims this "mountain lion" as her triumph in the name of Bakkhos. She bears his head into Thebes to present to her horrified father Kadmos (Bagg 1978: 55–63). Retribution has come with a gruesome reminder of the sacrificial economy in which all forms of life exist, killing and eating each other as shapes and living forms change in the act of nourishment. Dionysus embodies this kind of celebratory and simultaneously destructive interanimality, with its enmeshment in the plant world and the whole ecosystem. The refusal of Pentheus and his mother to acknowledge this sacred reality leads to their own sacrificial catastrophe.

As we have seen in these few examples, the semiotic scaffolding of human culture retains early forms of representation and expression upon which increasingly complex and sophisticated behaviors develop, adapted by their creators for the climates and biotic communities to which they respond. We now know that the Neolithic megaliths of Gavrinnis, Newgrange, Knowth, and Dowth were made by agrarian descendants of migrating Anatolian farmers who disappeared with the arrival of horse-riding Yamnaya warriors from Central Asia who swept into Europe between 4,000 and 5,000 years ago (Reich 2018: 106–121). Marija Gimbutas (1982) turned out to be right after all in asserting that what she called an Old European culture of relatively peaceful agriculturalists was displaced by a warrior society of horsemen and their chariots. Yet many earlier practices and beliefs remained beneath the surface of heroic myths, or they were awkwardly mingled with the new, more aggressive ways of thinking and the Indo–European mythic tradition that embodied them. These may have caused the kinds of tensions we encounter in works like *The Bacchae*. Similar discordant elements may exist in the Gilgamesh epic for the same reasons, although there are no mentions of horses or chariots in the Mesopotamian cuneiform narratives about Gilgamesh. This lack implies that the original cultural material behind the written texts may well be oral traditions that predate horse culture in the region.

Folk rituals of bull leaping and dancing are still performed in Spain and Southern France, reaching back to Minoan times and their depiction in frescoes on the walls of Knossos – perhaps even as far back as the baiting scenes on the walls of Çatalhöyük (e.g. "Bull acrobatics [Recortes], Pamplona" 2009; see Gimbutas [1982]: 196–199). In these performances, the bull is the hero and is never harmed. Men run around the bull, teasing him, taunting him, and then leaping over him as in the Minoan frescoes. In the Course Camarguaise still performed in many parts of Provence, many young men dressed in white run at angles across the bull's path, trying to snatch paper flowers and cords from between his horns. Those trophies win prizes, while the bull trots unharmed around the arena and the men leap over red wooden walls to escape him. Ancient seasonal rituals continue to be performed in folk festivals all over Europe – for example, Halloween (Celtic Samhain), Yuletide (Roman Saturnalia), St. John's fires (Beltaine), and harvest festivals (Lughnasa). Shakespeare based his plays on previous stories and dramas from medieval England as well as France and Italy, as in *Lear, Hamlet, Pericles*, and *Midsummer Night's Dream*. Since his time those stories and forms continue to be repeated and reshaped. They remain fully alive, if half-buried, like the stories of Homer and the Hebrew scriptures and similar traditional narratives in Asia such as the *Ramayana* in India, Indonesia, and Thailand. Fascination with powerful animals persists even in urbanized countries like the United States, where football teams have mascots and cartoonish human representatives such as Bulls, Hawks, Ravens, Lions, Bears, Tigers, Wolves, and Jaguars. Native American tribes continue to stage traditional dances invoking bison, turkeys, and ravens represented by men wearing horns and feathers. We are still haunted by our ancient relationships with creatures and landscapes that are fast approaching extinction, even though most people in so-called advanced countries live in concrete and steel urban environments far from independently thriving wild landscapes that continue to shrink.

Summary and Conclusion

This discussion has proceeded in four main sections. Section 1 seeks to establish the general place of modern humans (*Homo sapiens*) within the interconnected, dynamic matrix of life on Earth. Section 2 traces the emergence of the various hominin species of our ancestors to *Homo erectus* and its main descendants that led to modern humans. Section 3 concerns *Homo sapiens* and the development of culture stimulated by climate changes of the past 50,000 years up to the burst of Paleolithic cave art where we encounter, for the first time, the visions of people much like ourselves. Section 4 discusses Neolithic art and literature from the first monumental architecture and settled towns and cities, and anxiously considers the human relation to wild environments and other living beings.

Beginning with a reminder of the short span that *Homo sapiens* has existed in the dynamic and often violent life of the planet, Section 1 emphasizes the intricately interconnected web in which we coevolved with all other life-forms. Biosemiotics reveals the meaningful intercommunication at all levels and among all types of living things. Symbiosis is central to the emergence of life and its continuance in mutualisms such as plant networks and mimicry, as seen in the examples of pollination and the external forms of butterflies with eyespots or insects assuming the forms of twigs.

In Section 2, we follow the evolution of hominins within the interdependent matrix of plants and animals. Around 1.9 million years ago *Homo erectus* managed to spread over a huge span of Europe and Asia after migrating out of Africa. Key to this remarkable diffusion is a history of bipedalism and meat-eating, leading to larger brain size and cognitive development that allowed the creation of cultural technologies including stone tools, crude clothing, and the control of fire. These early ancestors created cultures and communicative forms in order to adapt to constantly changing environments within their plant and animal communities. Changing climates constantly shaped these cultural developments.

When we turn to fully modern humans in Section 3 of this exploration, we trace their overlapping and cohabitation with closely related other humans, such as Neanderthals and Denisovans, before emerging as the sole survivors of the genus *Homo* around 40,000 years ago. Modern humans began to record their visions of the world in art such as the great Paleolithic cave paintings of animals in Western Europe. Finally, in Section 4 we come to the Neolithic period when they settled in towns and began to domesticate plants and other animals. These developments were in part efforts to separate themselves from the world around them and to try to control it. Deep anxieties came with these new ways of life, as the first literatures reveal in examples such as the Gilgamesh epic and Euripides' *Bacchae*. In the big picture, such events are fairly recent, and those anxieties are still with us, haunting our dreams and imaginations.

Has this study been an elegy? With intricate and powerful global technologies that seem to insulate modern humans from most of the natural forces that shaped the history of our species, we are neither ready nor able to return to simpler lives that engage directly with the ecosystems and landscapes around us – yet these are drastically changing as the climate warms. None of us may be here to witness what is coming, but we must realize that the Anthropocene accompanies an illusion of control that is likely to collapse as the planet's life takes a dramatic new turn (see Lovelock 2006). We can only hope that some understanding of our deep past and our unending entanglement with other living creatures and forces leads enough humans to find survivable ways to adapt and redirect their cultural behaviors so that we and our biosphere companions can continue to live. Mars is not really an option.

References

Ackerman, J. 2020. *The Bird Way: A New Look at How Birds Talk, Work, Play, Parent, and Think*. New York: Penguin.

Allaby, R. G., L. Kistler, R. M. Gutaker, et al. 2015. "Archaeogenomic insights into the adaptation of plants to the human environment: pushing plant–hominin co-evolution back to the Pliocene." *Journal of Human Evolution* 79: 150–157. http://dx.doi.org/10.1016/j.jhevol.2014.10.014.

Alperson-Afil, N. 2017. "Spacial analysis of fire: archaeological approach to recognizing early fire." *Current Anthropology* 58 (S16): S258–S266. https://doi.org/10.1086/692721.

Ardetti, J. J. Elliott, I. J. Kitching, and L.T. Wasserthal. 2012. "'Good heavens what insect can suck it' – Charles Darwin, *Agraecum sesquipedale* and *Xathopan morganii Praedicta*." *Botanical Journal of the Linnean Society* 169: 403–432.

Armiero, M. 2021. *Wasteocene: Stories from the Global Dump*. Cambridge: Cambridge University Press.

Aubert, M., A. Brumm, M. Ramli, et al. 2014. "Pleistocene cave art from Sulawesi, Indonesia." *Nature* 514: 223–227. https://doi.org/10.1038/nature 13422.

Bagg, R. trans, 1978. *The Bakkhai by Euripides*. Amherst: University of Massachusetts Press.

Bar-Yosef, O. 1990. "The Natufian culture in the Levant, threshold to the origins of agriculture." *Evolutionary Anthropology* 4 (3): 159–177.

Barnard, P. 1987. "Foraging site selection by three raptors in relation to grassland burning in a montane habitat." *African Journal of Ecology* 25 (1): 35–45.

Bobe, R. and K. Behrensmeyer. 2004. "The expansion of grassland ecosystems in Africa in relation to mammalian evolution and the origin of the genus *Homo*." *Paleogeography, Paleoclimatology, Paleoecology* 207: 399–420.

Bonta, M., R. Gosford, D. Eussen, et al. 2017. "Intentional fire-spreading by 'firehawk' raptors in northern Australia." *Journal of Ethnobiology* 37 (4): 700–718.

Bramble, D. M. and D. E. Lieberman. 2004. "Endurance running and the evolution of *Homo*." *Nature* 432 (7015): 345–352. https://doi.org/10.1038/nature03052.

Bronstein, J. L., R. Alarcón, and M. Geber. 2006. "The evolution of plant–insect mutualisms." *New Phytologist* 172 (3): 412–428.

Brumm, A., A. A. Oktaviana, B. Burhan, et al. 2021. "Oldest cave art found in Sulawesi." *Science Advances* 7 (3). https://doi.org/10.1126/sciadv.abd4648.

"Bull acrobatics (Recortes), Pamplona." 2009. YouTube video. www.google.com/search?client=firefox-b-1-d&q=Bull+acrobatics%2CPamplona.

Callaway, E. 2016. "'Cave of forgotten dreams' may hold earliest painting of volcanic eruption." *Nature.* https://doi.org/10.1038/nature.2016.19177.

2017. "Oldest *Homo sapiens* fossil claim rewrites our species' history." *Nature*, June 7.

2022. "Evidence of Europe's first *Homo sapiens* found in French cave." *Nature.* https://doi.org/10.1038/d41586-022-00389-9.

Cardenal, E. 2013. *Versos del Pluriverso: Poemas que han sido añadidosa Cántico Cósmico.* Miami, FL: La Pereza Ediciones.

"Caterpillar mimics snake." 2016. YouTube video. www.google.com/search?client=firefox-b-1-d&q=You+Tube%2C+Caterpillar+Mimics+Snake.

Cauvin, J. 2000. *The Birth of the Gods and the Origins of Agriculture*, trans. T. Watkins. Cambridge: Cambridge University Press.

Chakrabarty, D. 2009. "The climate of history: four theses." *Critical Inquiry* 35: 201–207.

Chauvet, J.-M., E. B. Deschamps, C. Hillaire, J. Clottes, and P. G. Bahn. 1996. *Dawn of Art: The Chauvet Cave.* New York: Harry N. Abrams.

Clark, S. 2013. "Strange strangers and uncanny hammers: Morton's *The Ecological Thought* and the phenomenological tradition." *Green Letters: Studies in Ecocriticism* 13 (2): 98–108.

Clottes, J. and D. Lewis-Williams. 1998. *The Shamans of Prehistory: Trance and Magic in the Painted Caves*, trans. S. Hawkes. New York: Harry N. Abrams.

Conde-Valverde, M., I. Martínez, R. M. Quam, and M. Rosa-Zurera. 2021. "Neanderthals and *Homo sapiens* had similar auditory and speech capacities." *Nature Ecology & Evolution* 5: 609–615. https://doi.org/10.1038/s41559-021-01391-6.

Cook, J. 2013. *Ice Age Art: Arrival of the Modern Mind.* London: British Museum Press.

Coolidge, F. L. and T. Wynn. 2018. *The Rise of Homo Sapiens: The Evolution of Modern Thinking.* 2nd ed. Oxford: Oxford University Press.

Cunliffe, B. 2012. *Britain Begins.* Oxford: Oxford University Press.

2008. *Europe between the Oceans 9000–AD 1000.* New Haven, CT: Yale University Press.

Dalley, S. 1991. *Myths from Mesopotamia: Creation, The Flood, Gilgamesh, and Others*. Oxford: Oxford University Press.

Darwin, C. 1862. *On the Various Contrivances by Which British and Foreign Orchids Are Fertilised by Insects, and the Good Effects of Intercrossing*. London: John Murray.

1981. *The Descent of Man, and Sexual Selection in Relation to Sex*. Princeton, NJ: Princeton University Press. (Originally published in 1871.)

"Darwin's comet orchid." 2008. YouTube video. www.youtube.com/watch? v=OMVN1EWxfAU.

Davis-Marks, I. 2021. "120,000 year-old cattle bone carvings may be world's oldest surviving symbols." *Smithsonian Magazine*, February 8.

De Bona, S, J. K. Valkonen, A. López-Sepulcre, and J.Mappes. 2015. "Predator mimicry, not conspicuousness, explains the effacacy of butterfly eyespots." *Proceedings of the Royal Society B* 282: 20150202. https://doi .org/10.1098/rspb.2015.0202.

de Chardin, T. 1975. *The Phenomenon of Man*, trans. B. Wall with an Introduction by Sir Julian Huxley. New York: Harper & Row. (Originally published as *Le Phénomene Humain*. Paris: Editions de Seuil, 1955.)

DeSilva, J. 2021. *First Steps: How Upright Walking Made Us Human*. New York: HarperCollins.

Deacon, T. 1997. *The Symbolic Species: The Coevolution of Language and the Brain*. New York: Norton.

Dennell, R. 2009. *The Palaeolithic Settlement of Asia*. Cambridge: Cambridge University Press.

Descola, P. 2013. *Beyond Nature and Culture*, trans. J. Lloyd. Chicago, IL: University of Chicago Press. (Originally published as *Par-delá nature et culture*. Paris: Éditions Gallimard, 2005.)

Dodds, E. R. 1960. *Euripides Bacchae*, edited and with a commentary by E. R. Dodds. Oxford: Clarendon Press.

Douglas, A. E. 2010. *The Symbiotic Habit*. Princeton, NJ: Princeton University Press.

Dufourcq, A. 2022. *The Imaginary of Animals*. New York: Routledge.

Dunbar, R. 2004. *The Human Story*. London: Faber and Faber.

Fay, N., B. Walker, T. M. Elison, et al. 2022. "Gesture is the primary modality for language creation." *Royal Society Proceedings B*. https://doi.org/10 .1098/rspb.2022.0066.

Feldman, M. W. and K. N. Laland, 1996. "Gene-culture coevolutionary theory." *Tree* 11 (11): 453–457.

Feschotte, C. 2008. "Transposable elements and the evolution of regulatory networks." *Nature Reviews Genetics* 9: 397–405.

Finlayson, C. 2004. *Neanderthals and Modern Humans: An Ecological and Evolutionary Perspective*. Cambridge: Cambridge University Press.

Flannery, T. 2021. "Why did they vanish?" *The New York Review of Books* 18 (8): 28–29.

Fraser, D. 1966. "The heraldic woman: a study in diffusion," in *The Many Faces of Primitive Art*, ed. D. Fraser, 36–99. Englewood Cliffs, NJ: Prentice Hall.

George, A. R. 2003. *The Babylonian Gilgamesh Epic*. Oxford: Oxford University Press.

Ghose, Tina. 2016. "Why did ancient Europeans just disappear 14,500 years ago?" *Live Science*, March 1. www.livescience.com/53883-ancient-europeans-vanished-after-ice-age.html.

Gibbons, A. 2017. "World's oldest *Homo sapiens* fossils found in Morocco." *Science*, June 9. https://doi.org/10.1126/science.aan6934.

2021. "Stunning 'Dragon Man' skull may be an elusive Denisovan – or a new species of human." *Science*, June 25. www.science.org/content/article/stunning-dragon-man-skull-may-be-elusive-denisovan-or-new-species-human.

Gilligan, I. 2018. *Climate, Clothing, and Agriculture in Prehistory*. Cambridge: Cambridge University Press.

Gimbutas, M. 1982. *Goddesses and Gods of Old Europe*. Berkeley: University of California Press.

Gowlett, J. A. J. 2016. "The discovery of fire by humans: a long and convoluted process." *Philosophical Transactions B* 371: 20150164. http://dx.doi.org/10.1098/rstb.2015.0164.

Gresky, J., J. Helm, and L.Clare. 2017. "Modified human crania from Göbekli Tepe provide evidence for a new form of Neolithic skull cult." *Science Advances* 3 (6). https://doi.org/10.1126/sciadv.1700564.

Gron, Kurt J., J.Montgomery, and P.Rowly. 2015. "Cattle management for dairying in Scandinavia's earliest Neolithic. *PLoS ONE* 10 (7): e0131267. https://doi.org/10.1371/journal.pone.0131267.

Haile-Selassie, Y., S. M. Melillo, A. Vazzana, S. Benazzi, and T. M. Ryan. 2019. "A 3.8-million-year-old hominin cranium from Waronzo-Mille, Ethiopia." *Nature* 573: 214–219.

Harper, K. 2021. *Plagues upon the Earth: Disease and the Course of Human History*. Princeton, NJ: Princeton University Press.

Harrison, T. 2010. "Apes among the tangled branches of human origins." *Science* 327: 532–534.

Hattam, J. 2016. "What happened to Turkey's ancient utopia?" *Discover Magazine*, July 27.

Haws, J., M. M. Benedetti, S. Talamo, and B. K. Zinsious. 2020. "The early Aurignacian dispersal of modern humans into westernmost Eurasia." *PNAS* 117 (41): 25414–25422. https://doi.org10.1073/pnas.2016062117.

Hodder, I. 2006. *The Leopard's Tale: Revealing the Mysteries of Çatalhöyük.* London: Thames & Hudson.

2007. "Çatalhöyük in the context of the Middle Eastern Neolithic." *Annual Review of Anthropology* 36: 105–120.

Hoffmann, D. L., C. D. Standish, M. Garcia-Diaz, et al. 2018. "U-Th dating of carbonate crusts reveals Neandertal origin of Iberian cave art." *Science* 359: 912–915.

Hoffmeyer, J. 1996. *Signs of Meaning in the Universe*, trans. B. J. Haveland. Bloomington: Indiana University Press.

2008. *Biosemiotics: An Examination into the Signs of Life and the Life of Signs*, trans. J. Hoffmeyer and D. Favareau. Scranton, PA: University of Scranton Press. (Originally published as *Biosemiotik. Enafhandling om livets tegn og tegnenesliv.* Copenhagen: Ries Forlag, 2005.)

2015. "Semiotic scaffolding: a unitary principle gluing life and culture together." *Green Letters: Studies in Ecocriticism* (Special Issue: Biosemiotics and Culture, ed. W. Wheeler and L. Westling) 19: 243–254.

Huerta-Sánchez, E., X. Jin, Z. Asan Bianba, et al. 2014. "Altitude adaptation in Tibetans caused by introgression of Denisova-like DNA." *Nature* 512 (7513): 194–197. https://doi.org/10.1038/nature13408.

Husserl, E. 2013. "Addendum XXIII of *The Crisis of European Sciences and Transcendental Phenomenology*," trans. N. Keane. *Journal of the British Society for Phenomenology* 44 (6):6.

Imbler, S. 2021. "Before they spoke, they had to listen." *New York Times*, March 9.

Ingold, T. 2000. *The Perception of the Environment: Essays on Livelihood, Dwelling and Skill.* London: Routledge.

Iovino, S. 2021. *Italo Calvino's Animals: Anthropocene Stories.* Cambridge: Cambridge University Press.

Jacobson-Tepfer, E. 2015. *The Hunter, the Stag, and the Mother of Animals: Image, Monument, and Landscape in North Asia.* New York: Oxford University Press.

2020. *The Anatomy of Deep Time: Rock Art and Landscape in the Altai Mountains of Mongolia.* Cambridge: Cambridge University Press.

Kleisner, K. 2008. "The semantic morphology of Adolf Portmann: a starting point for the biosemiotics of organic form?" *Biosemiotics* 1: 207–219. https://doi.org10.1007/s12304-008-9014-4.

La course landaise – "bull-dancing" in Vieux Boucau. 2010. YouTube video. www.youtube.com/watch?v=-0mJXIMioPw.

Leakey, L. L. 1974. *By the Evidence: Memoirs 1932–1951*. New York: Harcourt Brace Jovanovich.

Leakey, M. D. 1979. *Olduvai Gorge: My Search for Early Man*. London: Collins.

Leakey, M. G., with S. Leakey. 2020. *The Sediments of Time: My Lifelong Search for the Past*. New York: Houghton Mifflin Harcourt.

Leakey, M. G., C. S. Feibel, I. McDougall, and A. Walker. 1995. "New four-million-year-old hominid species from Kanapoi and Allia Bay, Kenya." *Nature* 376: 565–571.

Leakey, M. G., C. S. Feibel, I. McDougall, C. Ward, and A. Walker. 1998. "New specimens and confirmation of an early age for *Australopithecus anamensis*." *Nature* 393: 62–66.

Leakey, R. E. 1994. *The Origins of Humankind*. New York: Basic Books.

Leroi-Gouran, A. 1967. *Treasures of Prehistoric Art*, trans. N. Guterman. New York: Harry N. Abrams.

Lewontin, R. 2000. *The Triple Helix: Gene, Organism, and Environment*. Cambridge, MA: Harvard University Press.

Lieberman, D. E., B. M.McBratney, and G.Krovitz. 2002. "The evolution and development of cranial form in *Homo sapiens*." *PNAS* 99 (3): 1134–1139. https://doi.org/10.1073/pnas.022440799.

Littman, R. J. 2009. "The plague of Athens: epidemiology and paleopathology." *Mount Sinai Journal of Medicine*. https://doi.org/10.1002/msj.20137.

Lotman, J. and W. Clark. 2005. "On the semiosphere." *Semiotica: Sign Systems Studies* 13 (1): 205–226. https://doi.org/10.12697/SSS.2005.33.1.09. (Originally published in Russian as *Sign Systems Studies*, 1984.)

Lovelock, J. 2006. *The Revenge of Gaia: Earth's Climate Crisis and the Fate of Humanity*. New York: Basic Books.

Maher, L. A. and M. Conkey. 2019. "Homes for hunters? Exploring the concept of home at hunter–gatherer sites in Upper Paleolithic Europe and Epipaleolithic Southwest Asia." *Current Anthropology* 60 (1): 91–137.

Maran, T. 2015. "Scaffolding and mimicry: a semiotic view of the evolutionary dynamics of mimicry systems." *Biosemiotics* 8: 211–222.

2020. *Ecosemiotics: The Study of Signs in Changing Ecologies*. Cambridge: Cambridge University Press.

Maran, T. and K. Kull. 2014. "Ecosemiotics: main principles and current developments." *Geografiska Annaler: Series B, Human Geography* 96 (1): 41–50.

Margulis, L. 1998. *Symbiotic Planet: A New View of Evolution*. New York: Basic Books.

Marshack, A. 1972. *The Roots of Civilization*. New York: McGraw Hill.

Matz, F. 1962. *La Crète et la Grèce Primitive*. Paris: Éditions Albin Michel.

Max-Planck-Gesellschaft. 2019. "First hominins on the Tibetan Plateau were Denisovans." *Science Daily*, May 1. www.sciencedaily.com/releases/2019/05/190501131405.htm.

Mellaart, J. 1966. *The Chalcolithic and Early Bronze Ages in the Near East and Anatolia*. Beirut: Khayats.

1970. *Excavations at Hacilar (2)*. Edinburgh: The British Institute of Archaeology at Ankara.

1975. *The Neolithic of the Near East*. New York: Scribner's.

Merleau-Ponty, M. 1973. *The Visible and the Invisible* (followed by working notes), ed. C. Lefort, trans. A. Lingis. Evanston, IL: Northwestern University Press.

2003. *Nature: Course Notes from the Collège de France*, compiled and with notes by D. Séglard, trans. R. Vallier. Evanston, IL: Northwestern University Press. (Originally published as *La Nature: Notes, cours du Collège de France*, 1995.)

Mithen, S. 2003. *After the Ice: A Global Human History 20,000–5000 BC*. Cambridge, MA: Harvard University Press.

Morton, T. 2010. *The Ecological Thought*. Cambridge, MA: Harvard University Press.

Musée d'"Archéologie Nationale. 2021. *Lascaux*. Video. https://archeologie.culture.fr/lascaux/en.

Museum Staff. n.d. *The Museum of Anatolian Civilizations*. Ankara: The Association for the Support and Encouragement of the Museum of Anatolian Civilizations.

Neubaur, S., N.-J. Hublin, and P.Gunz. 2018. "The evolution of modern human brain shape." *Science Advances* 4:1. https://doi.org/10.1126/sciadv.aao5961.

Nilsson, M. A. 1932. *The Mycenaean Origin of Greek Mythology*. Berkeley: University of California Press.

Noble, D. 2017. *Dance to the Tune of Life: Biological Relativity*. Cambridge: Cambridge University Press.

Nomade, S., D. Genty, R. Sasco, et al. 2016. "A 36,000 year old volcanic eruption depicted in the Chauvet-Pont d'Arc cave (Ardèche, France)?" *PLoS ONE* 11 (1): e0146621. https://doi.org/10.1371/journal.pone.0146621.

Odling-Smee, J., K. Laland, and M.Feldman. 2003. *Niche Construction: The Neglected Process in Evolution.* Princeton, NJ: Princeton University Press.

Oskin, B. 2013. "9,000-year-old painting of volcano linked to a real eruption." *NBC Science News,* October 30.

Pace, J. K. II and C. Feschotte. 2007. "The evolutionary history of human DNA transposons: evidence for intense activity in the primate lineage." *Genome Research* 17 (4): 422–432.

Papagianni, D. and M. A. Morse. 2015. *The Neanderthals Rediscovered: How Modern Science Is Rewriting Their Story.* London: Thames & Hudson.

Pascoe, B. 2018. *Dark Emu: Aboriginal Australia and the Birth of Agriculture.* London: Scribe.

Peris, J., V. B. Gonzalez, R. Blasco, et al. 2012. "The earliest evidence of hearths in Southern Europe: The case of Balomor Cave (Valencia, Spain)." *Quarternary International,* 247: 267–277. https://doi.org/10.1016/j.quaint.2010.10.014.

Peyre Blanque Project. www.peyreblanque.org.

Portmann, A. 1967. *Animal Forms and Patterns: A Study of the Appearance of Animals.* New York: Schocken Books. (Originally published as *Die Tiergestalt,* 1948.)

Potts, S. G., C. Kremen, P.Neumann, O. Schweiger, and W. E. Kunin. 2010. "Global pollinator declines: trends, impacts and drivers." *Trends in Ecology and Evolution* 25 (6): 345–353.

Quammen, D. 2018. *The Tangled Tree: A Radical New History of Life.* New York: Simon & Schuster.

Rabett, R. J. 2012. *Human Adaptation in the Asian Palaeolithic: Hominin Dispersal and Behaviour during the Late Quaternary.* Cambridge: Cambridge University Press.

Raia, P., A. Mondanaro, M. Melchionna, et al. 2020. "Past extinctions of *Homo* species coincided with increased vulnerability to climate change." *One Earth* 3 (4): 480–490. https://doi.org/10.1016/j.oneear.2020.09.007.

Reich, D. 2018. *Who We Are and How We Got Here: Ancient DNA and the New Science of the Human Past.* New York: Pantheon.

Reich, D., N. Patterson, M. Kircher, et al. 2011. "Denisova admixture and the first modern human dispersals into Southeast Asia and Oceana." *American Journal of Human Genetics* 89(4): 516–528. https://doi.org/10.1016/j.ajhg.2011.09.005.

Richerson, P. J., R. Boyd, and J.Heinrich. 2010. "Gene-culture coevolution in the age of genomics." *PNAS* 107: 8985–8992.

Rizal, Y., K. A. Westaway, Y. Zaim, et al. 2020. "Last appearance of *Homo erectus* at Ngandong, Java, 117,000–108,000 years ago." *Nature* 577: 381–385. https://doi.org/10.1038/s41586-019-1863-2.

Robinson, J. 1992. "Not counting on Marshack; a reassessment of the work of Alexander Marshack on notation in the Upper Paleolithic." *Journal of Mediterranean Studies* 2 (1): 1–16.

Safina, C. 2015. *Beyond Words: What Animals Think and Feel.* New York: Henry Holt & Co.

Schleidt, W. and M. D. Shalter. 2003. "Co-evolution of humans and canids: an alternative view of dog domestication: Homo homini lupus?" *Evolution and Cognition* 9(1): 57–72.

Schmidt, K. 2007. *Göbekli Tepe: A Stone Age Sanctuary in South-East Anatolia.* Berlin: ex oriente e. V. (Originally published as *Sie bauten die ersten Tempel.* München: C.H. Beck, 2006.)

Sharov, A, T. Maran, and M.Tønnessen. 2015. "Organisms reshape sign relations." *Biosemiotics* 8: 361–365. https://doi.org/10.1007/s12304-015-9251-2.

Shryock, A. and D. L. Smail, eds. 2011. *Deep History: The Architecture of Past and Present.* Berkeley: University of California Press.

Simard, S. W. 2012. "Mycorrhizal networks and seedling establishment in Douglas-fir forests," in *Biocomplexity of Plant–Fungal Interactions*, ed. D. Southworth, 85–107.Ames, IA: Wiley-Blackwell.

2018. "Mycorrhizal networks facilitate tree communication, learning and memory," in *Memory and Learning in Plants*, eds. F. Baluška, M. Gagliano, and G. Witzany, 191–213. West Sussex, UK: Springer.

2021. *Finding the Mother Tree: Discovering the Wisdom of the Forest.* New York: Knopf.

Simard, S. W., K. J. Beiler, M. A.Bingham, et al. 2012. 'Mycorrhizal Networks: Mechanisms, Ecology, and Modeling." *Fungal Biology Reviews* 26 (1): 29–60.

Simard, S. W., K.Martin, A. Vyse, and B. Larson. 2013. "Meta-networks of fungi, fauna and flora as agents of complex adaptive systems," in *Managing World Forests as Complex Adaptive Systems: Building Resilience to the Challenge of Global Change*, eds. K. J. Puettmann, C. Messier, and K. D. Coates, 133–164. New York: Routledge.

Simard, S. W., A.Asay, K.Beiler, et al. 2015. "Resource transfer between plants through ectomycorrhizal fungal networks," in *Mycorrhizal Networks*, ed. T. R. Horton, 133–176. Dordrecht: Springer.

Slon, V., F. Mafessoni, B. Vernot, et al. 2018. "The genome of the offspring of a Neanderthal mother and a Denisovan father." *Nature* 561: 113–116. https://doi.org/10.1038/s41586.018-0455x.

Smail, D. L. 2008. *On Deep History and the Human Brain.* Berkeley: University of California Press.

Smith, S. 2015. "Green Arabia's key role in human evolution." *BBC News,* September 16.

Smithsonian National Museum of Human History. 2021. *"Homo heidelbergensis."* https://humanorigins.si.edu/evidence/human-fossils/species/homo-heidelbergensis.

St. Clair, K. 2018. *The Golden Thread: How Fabric Changed History.* New York: Liveright.

Strickland, A. 2018. "11,000 years ago, our ancestors survived abrupt climate change." *CNN,* March 30. www.cnn.com/2018/03/26/health/climate-change-hunter-gatherers.

Sykes, R. W. 2020. *Kindred: Neanderthal Life, Love, Death, and Art.* London: Bloomsbury Sigma.

The Oxford Classical Dictionary, eds. N. G. L. Hammond and H. H. Scullard. 1970. New York: Oxford University Press.

Todd, I. A. 1976. *Çatal Höyük in Perspective.* Menlo Park, CA: Cummings Publishing Company.

Van Arsdale, A. P. 2013. *"Homo erectus* - A bigger, faster hominin lineage." *Nature Education Knowledge* 4 (1): 2.

von Petzinger, G. 2016. *The First Signs: Unlocking the Mysteries of the World's Oldest Symbols.* New York: Simon & Schuster.

von Uexküll, J. 1934. *A Stroll Through the Worlds of Animals and Men: A Picture Book of Invisible Worlds.* (Published online 2009 – https://doi.org/10.1515/semi.1992.89.4.319.)

Vrba, E., G. H.Denton, T. C. Partridge, and L.Burkle, eds. 1995. *Paleoclimate and Evolution, with Emphasis on Human Origins.* New Haven, CT: Yale University Press.

Wagner, D. L., E. M. Grames, M. L. Forister, M. R. Berenbaum, and D. Stopak. 2021. "Insect decline in the Anthropocene: death by a thousand cuts." *PNAS* 118 (2): e2023989118. https://doi.org/10.1073/pnas.2023989118.

Walker, E. A. 2017. "Paleolithic archaeology of Wales: overview," in *Encyclopedia of Global Archaeology,* ed. C. Smith. Springer: Cham. https://doi.org/10.1007/978-3-319-51726-1_2138-2.

Ward, P. and J.Kirschvink. 2015. *A New History of Life: The Radical New Discoveries about the Origins and Evolution of Life on Earth.* London: Bloomsbury Press.

Westling, L. 2014. *The Logos of the Living World: Merleau-Ponty, Animals, and Language.* New York: Fordham University Press.

2018. "Deep history, interspecies coevolution, and the eco-imaginary," in *Exploring Animal Encounters: Philosophical, Cultural, and Historical*

Perspectives, eds. D. Ohrem and M. Calarco, 209–231. Palgrave Macmillan: Cham, Switzerland.

2021. "Human–animal relations in Neolithic Anatolian art: the heritage of the bull," in *Turkish Ecocriticism*, eds. S. Opperman and S. Akilli, 131–147. London: Lexington Books.

Wheeler, W. 2006. *The Whole Creature: Complexity, Biosemiotics, and the Evolution of Culture*. London: Lawrence & Wishart.

2016. *Expecting the Earth: Life, Culture, Biosemiotics*. London: Lawerence and Wishart.

Yong, E. 2016. *I Contain Multitudes: The Microbes within Us and a Grander View of Life*. New York: HarperCollins.

Acknowledgments

Versions of material in three sections of this Element have appeared previously. An earlier and somewhat differently focused discussion of *The Epic of Gilgamesh* and Euripides' *Bakkhai* appeared on pages 49–60 of my book, *The Logos of the Living World: Merleau-Ponty, Animals, and Language* (2014). It is presented here with the kind permission of Fordham University Press. I have also reshaped ideas presented in "Deep history, interspecies coevolution, and the eco-imaginary," pages 209–231 of *Exploring Animal Encounters: Philosophical, Cultural, and Historical Perspectives*, edited by Dominik Ohrem and Matthew Calarco (2018), reproduced with the permission of Palgrave Macmillan. Lexington Books has granted permission to reprint material from my chapter "Human–animal relations in Neolithic Anatolian art: the heritage of the bull," pages 131–147 in Serpil Oppermann and Sinan Akilli's coedited collection, *Turkish Ecocriticism: From Neolithic to Contemporary Timescapes*, Lexington Books (2021), all rights reserved.

Cambridge Elements ≡

Environmental Humanities

Louise Westling
University of Oregon

Louise Westling is an American scholar of literature and environmental humanities who was a founding member of the Association for the Study of Literature and Environment and its President in 1998. She has been active in the international movement for environmental cultural studies, teaching and writing on landscape imagery in literature, critical animal studies, biosemiotics, phenomenology, and deep history.

Serenella Iovino
University of North Carolina at Chapel Hill

Serenella Iovino is Professor of Italian Studies and Environmental Humanities at the University of North Carolina at Chapel Hill. She has written on a wide range of topics, including environmental ethics and ecocritical theory, bioregionalism and landscape studies, ecofeminism and posthumanism, comparative literature, eco-art, and the Anthropocene.

Timo Maran
University of Tartu

Timo Maran is an Estonian semiotician and poet. Maran is Professor of Ecosemiotics and Environmental Humanities and Head of the Department of Semiotics at the University of Tartu. His research interests are semiotic relations of nature and culture, Estonian nature writing, zoosemiotics and species conservation, and semiotics of biological mimicry.

About the Series

The environmental humanities is a new transdisciplinary complex of approaches to the embeddedness of human life and culture in all the dynamics that characterize the life of the planet. These approaches reexamine our species' history in light of the intensifying awareness of drastic climate change and ongoing mass extinction. To engage this reality, Cambridge Elements in Environmental Humanities builds on the idea of a more hybrid and participatory mode of research and debate, connecting critical and creative fields.

Cambridge Elements ≡

Environmental Humanities

Printed in the United States
by Baker & Taylor Publisher Services